FORGOTTEN GOD

FORGOTTEN GOD
REVERSING OUR TRAGIC NEGLECT OF THE HOLY SPIRIT

FRANCIS CHAN
with Danae Yankoski

David C. Cook®

transforming lives together

FORGOTTEN GOD
Published by David C. Cook
4050 Lee Vance View
Colorado Springs, CO 80918 U.S.A.

David C. Cook Distribution Canada
55 Woodslee Avenue, Paris, Ontario, Canada N3L 3E5

David C. Cook U.K., Kingsway Communications
Eastbourne, East Sussex BN23 6NT, England

David C. Cook and the graphic circle C logo
are registered trademarks of Cook Communications Ministries.

The Web site addresses recommended throughout this book are offered as a
resource to you. These Web sites are not intended in any way to be or imply an
endorsement on the part of David C. Cook, nor do we vouch for their content.

ISBN 978-1-61129-881-9

Published in association with the literary agency of
D.C. Jacobson & Associates LLC, an Author Management Company

The Team: John Blase, Amy Kiechlin, Sarah Schultz, Caitlyn York, and Karen Athen
Cover Design: The Regime, Jim Elliston

Printed in the United States of America

To Rachel,
My daughter and friend:

You have no idea how happy I am to see the Spirit alive in you.
Let's follow Him together, forever.

CONTENTS

FORGOTTEN GOD

ACKNOWLEDGMENTS

Lisa and the kids—for supporting me as I seek to take our family wherever the Spirit leads. I know it's not always easy.

The elders of Cornerstone Church—for your patient and Spirit-led instruction in my life. I love serving alongside you.

Danae—Once again, I wouldn't have been able to do this without you. Your gift is obvious, and I admire your commitment to true, biblical Christianity.

Don and Jenni at D.C. Jacobson & Associates—for your guidance.

The team at David C. Cook—for all your work.

Jim—for designing such a cool cover. Everyone should buy a Web site from www.CloverSites.com. (You owe me a lot of sushi for that advertisement.)

Jesse and Reesh, Keith and Kristi, Gene and Sandra, Chris and Julie, Jim and Sherry, Ted and Sandy, Frank and Christy, Adam and Steph, Bill and Kathleen, Brice and Shelene, Mark and Jen, Doug and Frani, Kevin, Paul, Rochelle, and Susan. You guys didn't really help with anything, but you're good friends, and it's always fun to see your name in print.

INTRODUCTION

You might think that calling the Holy Spirit the "forgotten God" is a bit extreme. Maybe you agree that the church has focused too much attention elsewhere but feel it is an exaggeration to say we have *forgotten* about the Spirit. I don't think so.

From my perspective, the Holy Spirit is tragically neglected and, for all practical purposes, forgotten. While no evangelical would deny His existence, I'm willing to bet there are millions of churchgoers across America who cannot confidently say they have experienced His presence or action in their lives over the past year. And many of them do not believe they can.

The benchmark of success in church services has become more about attendance than the movement of the Holy Spirit. The "entertainment" model of church was largely adopted in the 1980s and '90s, and while it alleviated some of our boredom for a couple of hours a week, it filled our churches with self-focused consumers rather than self-sacrificing servants attuned to the Holy Spirit.

Perhaps we're too familiar and comfortable with the current state of the church to feel the weight of the problem. But what if you grew up on a desert island with nothing but the Bible to read? Imagine being rescued after twenty years and then attending a typical evangelical church. Chances are you'd be shocked (for a whole lot of reasons, but that is another story). Having read the Scriptures outside the context of contemporary church culture, you would be convinced that the Holy Spirit is as essential to a believer's existence as air is to staying alive. You would know that the Spirit led the first Christians to do unexplainable things, to live lives that didn't make sense to the culture around them, and ultimately to spread the story of God's grace around the world.

There is a big gap between what we read in Scripture about the Holy Spirit and how most believers and churches operate today. In many modern churches, you would be stunned by the apparent absence of the Spirit in any manifest way. And this, I believe, is the crux of the problem.

If I were Satan and my ultimate goal was to thwart God's kingdom and purposes, one of my main strategies would be to get churchgoers to ignore the Holy Spirit. The degree to which this has happened (and I would argue that it is a prolific disease in the body of Christ) is directly connected to the dissatisfaction most of us feel with and in the church. We understand something very important is missing. The feeling is so strong that some have run away from the church and God's Word completely.

I believe that this missing *something* is actually a missing *Someone*—namely, the Holy Spirit. Without Him, people operate in their own strength and only accomplish human-size results. The world is not moved by love or actions that are of human creation. And the church is not empowered to live differently from any other gathering of people without the Holy Spirit. But when believers live in the power of the Spirit, the evidence in their lives is supernatural. The church cannot help but be different, and the world cannot help but notice.

As I wrote this book, the question that kept burning in my mind was how can any human being write well on the sacred topic of the Holy Spirit of God? No subject intimidates me more, yet I can't think of anything more essential for God's church everywhere, and especially in the western hemisphere where it seems that the Holy Spirit is all but missing from most of our churches. I am most definitely writing from a western context, and I know that the body of Christ is vibrant and growing and the Holy Spirit active on continents like Africa, South America, and Asia. I also know that God works uniquely in various places and times, and I do think this explains part of the difference between here and there. However, I also believe that the Spirit is more obviously active in places where people are desperate for Him, humbled before Him, and not distracted by their pursuit of wealth or comforts (like we are).

The light of the American church is flickering and nearly extinguished, having largely sold out to the kingdoms and values of this world. While most people see that there is a problem, few do anything about it, and most of those who do, run toward the wrong solutions. Instead of speaking meaningfully and insightfully into the culture, we have capitulated and in many cases look no different from the world. I'm not sure if it is a calling or a sense of pure urgency that leads me to write this. Maybe both. The fact is, I don't have the "right" to write this book, but I believe it is a book that needs to be written, so I have written it, trusting that God will use it for His glory.

The Holy Spirit is absolutely vital to our situation today. Of course, He is always vital; but perhaps especially now. After all, if the Holy Spirit moves, nothing can stop Him. If He doesn't move, we will not produce genuine fruit—no matter how much effort or money we expend. The church becomes irrelevant when it becomes purely a human creation. We are not all we were made to be when everything in our lives and churches can be explained apart from the work and presence of the Spirit of God.

———

Perhaps it's not theology we're missing, but rather theological *integrity*. Many have the knowledge but lack the courage to admit the discrepancy between what we know and how we live. Hundreds of scholarly theological books have been written on the doctrine of the Holy Spirit, the doctrine of the Trinity, et cetera. This book is not one of those. *Obvious, neglected,* and *crucial* are the adjectives I would use to describe the truths I will present.

In the following chapters, I will explore the fundamental knowl-edge most of us have about the Holy Spirit. We will delve into some key Scriptures about the Holy Spirit and look at our own abuses, misconceptions, and even fears of Him. By journeying honestly, I hope we can go beyond our current understanding of the Holy Spirit and begin to commune openly … that our experience with Him would be day by day, even moment by moment. That by keeping in step with the Spirit, we might regularly fellowship over what He's *doing* rather than what He *did* months or years ago. We'll be reminded of the strength and wisdom available to us in the Spirit and earnestly pray for more. As we trust in the promises of the Spirit, we will be led away from discouragement and into lives marked by confidence, power in the midst of our weakness, and the fruit of the Spirit.

My prayer is that your changed life would produce this kind of astonishment: "Now when they saw the boldness of Peter and John, and perceived that they were uneducated, common men, they were *astonished*. And they recognized that they had been with Jesus" (Acts 4:13).

Reading this book probably won't be easy. No matter what religious tradition you come from, you likely carry baggage and harbor stereotypes when it comes to the Holy Spirit. It's going to require laying aside your baggage and stereotypes so you can be open to what God wants to teach you. Are you willing to do that?

Some of you hear the term *Holy Spirit* and automatically worry that I am going to get wildly charismatic on you. Others think of extreme conservatives who never acknowledge the Holy Spirit in word or deed and hope I'm not going there. There are a lot of stereotypes (some of which are true) and a lot of abuses, and they don't come from just one side of this issue.

Some people talk a lot about—even boast of—the Spirit, but their lives do not bear His fruit. Others speak of the Holy Spirit in theoretical or scholarly terms, yet do not experience Him at work. Still others ignore Him for all practical purposes and, as you might expect, rarely experience relationship or intimacy with the Spirit. And then there is that rare person who *doesn't* talk frequently about the Spirit, yet whose life is a powerful display of His presence and activity.

Some of you would like it if I said we were going to find a healthy balance between unhealthy extremes. That's not what we're going to do. When we are referring to God, balance is a huge mistake. God is not just one thing we add to the mix called life. He wants an invitation from us to permeate everything and every part of us. In the same way, seeking a "healthy balance" of the Holy Spirit assumes that there are some who have too much Holy Spirit and others who have too little. I have yet to meet *anyone* with too much Holy Spirit. Granted, I've met many who talk about Him too much, but none who are actually overfilled with His presence.

Is it possible to get enough or even too much God? Is there a point when a person can be satisfied with the amount of intimacy, knowledge, and power of God he or she experiences? I don't see how there can be, because doesn't every encounter with God only cause us to thirst for Him more?

Let me be clear. This is not a call to misinformed extremism, but an acknowledgment that as believers we can never be "done" with

God. He is infinite and we are finite; there will always be more of His character to discover, more of His love to experience, and more of His power to use for His purposes.

I can't say exactly what will happen when you admit that you can never fully know or experience enough of the Holy Spirit yet choose to seek Him regardless. I know only that when you surrender fully to the Spirit, Christ will be magnified, not you (John 16:14).

And perhaps the core issue is really about our holding back from giving ourselves to God, rather than our getting "too much" of Him. Perhaps when a person says, "I'd just like a little God, thank you very much," she or he is really saying, "I'd rather not give the parts of my life that I really care about over to God, so I'll just hold on to this, that, oh, and that, too…."

It doesn't work that way. When I read Scripture, I see the truth and necessity of a life wholly surrendered to and dependent upon the Holy Spirit.

Paul wrote to the Corinthians that his words were not "wise and persuasive" but rather a "demonstration of the Spirit's power" in order that their faith "might not rest on men's wisdom, but on God's power" (1 Cor. 2:4–5 NIV). Later in the same letter he reiterates that "the kingdom of God is not a matter of talk but of power" (4:20 NIV).

In most churches today I hear a lot of talk and the facade of human wisdom, but I don't see much of God's presence and power. Do you?

I am tired of merely talking about God. I want to see God move through me, through Cornerstone Church, and through the worldwide body of Christ. I know there's more. We all know there's more. That's why I wrote this book—to explore with you how God has called us to more, through the presence and strength of the Holy Spirit.

I refuse to live the remainder of my life where I am right now, stagnating at this point. Don't get me wrong: God has already done so much in my life, and I am grateful for it. I'm just convinced there's more. There's more of the Spirit and more of God than any of us is experiencing. I want to go there—not just intellectually, but in life, with everything that I am.

As we begin this book, may our desire to experience more of the Holy Spirit be our starting point. And may we open our hearts and lives to His presence and action more fully than we have ever done before. By the power and presence of the Holy Spirit, may we be different people when we finish from when we started.

ABOUT THE COVER

My friend Jim, who serves as one of the worship pastors at Cornerstone Church, designed the cover of this book after a message I gave about the difference between *exegesis* and *eisegesis*. It was one of the first lessons I learned in seminary.

Exegesis: an attempt to discover the meaning of the text objectively, starting with the text and moving out from there.

Eisegesis: to import a subjective, preconceived meaning into the text.

I was taught to interpret the Scriptures through exegesis alone. Start with God's Word; pray that the Spirit gives you clarity; then study to see what the text actually says. The Holy Spirit inspired the writing of the Bible, so who better to help us as we seek to understand it? Scripture tells us that the Spirit not only inspired the Bible, but also illumines it for us today (1 Cor. 2:12–16 and 2 Tim. 3:16).

The word *exegesis* comes from a Greek word meaning "to lead out." As I have said, you start with the text and draw out its meaning. Eisegesis, on the other hand, is when you start with an idea or conviction, then search for verses in the Bible to prove your point. I was warned against eisegesis, and rightly so. The danger in this is that we can take verses out of context to support just about any point of view. For years people have used this style of interpretation in order to justify greed, lust, divorce, and countless other sins. Cults also use eisegesis to justify their beliefs. After realizing this, we at Cornerstone began to question whether there were any areas in our lives where we did essentially the same thing.

The bottom line is that we can easily pursue just about any lifestyle we desire, then find Scriptures to show everyone it's all right to live that way. But what would it look like to live *exegetically?* If we were to start with Scripture and allow it to dictate our actions, how would we live?

I believe many people have an eisegetically formed concept of the Holy Spirit. In essence, we have cut and pasted whatever verses and ideas work for us; this forms our understanding of the Holy Spirit. The last thing I want to do is cut and paste a little more by giving you *my* "version" of the Holy Spirit. In this book, I endeavor to present the core truths that have been revealed to believers about the Holy Spirit—the things a Spirit-filled believer would conclude if he or she started with the Scriptures and proceeded from there.

CHAPTER 1

I've Got Jesus. Why Do I Need the Spirit?

> *We may as well face it: the whole level of spirituality*
> *among us is low. We have measured ourselves by ourselves*
> *until the incentive to seek higher plateaus in the things of*
> *the Spirit is all but gone.... [We] have imitated the world,*
> *sought popular favor, manufactured delights to substitute*
> *for the joy of the Lord and produced a cheap and synthetic*
> *power to substitute for the power of the Holy Ghost.*
>
> -A. W. Tozer-

I am convinced there is a desperate need in the church for the Holy Spirit of God to be given room to have His way. I think we can agree that there is a problem in our churches, that something is wrong. But I don't think we can reach an agreement on what to do about it. Most people do not connect what is missing or wrong with a particular need for the Holy Spirit.

A while back, our lack of openness to examining ourselves—especially in the area of the Holy Spirit—really hit me. Two Jehovah's Witnesses knocked on my door and initiated conversation. I had a lot to do, so I prepared to send them on their way. But as they began their spiel, I decided to take a few minutes and engage them. I gently told them that I found their teachings about Jesus offensive because they taught that Jesus was the same person as Michael the archangel. I told them that I believe He is much more than one among many angels; that I believe He is God. My visitors replied, "No, Jesus/Michael is the *only* archangel. There are no other archangels." So I asked them to open their Bibles to Daniel 10:13, which reads, "But the prince of the Persian kingdom resisted me twenty-one days. Then Michael, *one of* the chief princes, came to help me" (NIV). I pointed out that this passage is clear: Michael is only "one of" the chief princes (or archangels).

This caught them off guard. They told me they'd never heard or read this before. Now that I had their attention, I said, "There's no way you can look me in the eyes and tell me that you sat down one day seeking to find God, read the Bible, and came to the conclusion that Jesus is the same person as Michael the archangel. No one could come to that conclusion. You only believe it because that's what you were told, and I don't want to stand here and spoon-feed you something else." With that, I challenged them to read the Bible for themselves, rather than simply accept what they've been told about it. They went away that day and said they would consider doing that.

I left that conversation feeling a bit proud of myself because I stumped them and got them to question their beliefs. Yet I couldn't help but wonder whether I was fair to them. Had *I* ever sat down with the Bible and sought after its self-evident truth? Or had I passively ingested what I heard from other people, much like my front-door visitors?

It was then that I began reading the Scriptures as though I had never read them before. I asked the Spirit to make them "living and active" to me, though I'd been reading them for years. I asked God to "penetrate" the wrong and ill-conceived notions I'd collected along the way (Heb. 4:12 NIV). It's a great exercise for those of us who have been immersed in church culture for years.

There are, of course, dangers in this, since the Bible is meant to be interpreted within the context and accountability of faithful community. Yet even with that qualification, there is still a need for those of us nestled deep within the Christian bubble to look beyond the status quo and critically assess the degree to which we are really living biblically.

Most of us assume that what we believe is right (of course we do—it is why we believe what we believe) but have never really studied for ourselves. We were simply told, "This is the way it is," and didn't question. The problem is much of what we believe is often based more on comfort or our culture's tradition than on the Bible.

I believe we need to reexamine our faith just as much as the Jehovah's Witnesses who came to my door need to reconsider theirs. Remember, the Bereans were lifted up as good examples because they questioned the things they were taught. They made sure that even the apostles' teachings were in line with what was written: "Now the Bereans were of more noble character than the Thessalonians, for they received the message with great eagerness and examined the Scriptures every day to see if what Paul said was true" (Acts 17:11 NIV).

One of the areas we desperately need to examine is how we think about and relate to the Holy Spirit. As I said previously, if you or I had never been to a church and had read only the Old and New Testaments, we would have significant expectations of the Holy Spirit in our lives.

Think about it. Upon foretelling His death, Jesus comforts the disciples by telling them that "another Counselor" is coming (John 14:16 NIV). In John 16:7 He goes so far as to say it is to their *advantage* that He leave so the Counselor can come. And in Acts 1:4–5, after His death and resurrection, He tells His disciples to stay in Jerusalem and wait for the Holy Spirit. (The disciples obey because that's what people do when someone rises from the dead and gives instructions.) Jesus' disciples had no idea what or whom they were waiting for, or what it would be like. But they were expectant and trusting because Jesus had instructed them to wait for this good gift.

Then in Acts 2, we see the fulfillment of this promise in a way that must have shocked the disciples. The Holy Spirit's power is unleashed like no one had ever seen or experienced before, and Peter shares the amazing promise that this Holy Spirit is available to anyone who believes. The Epistles tell us of the Holy Spirit's amazing power at work in us, our Spirit-enabled ability to put our sin to death through Him, and the supernatural gifts He gives us.

If we read and believed these accounts, we would expect a great deal of the Holy Spirit. He would not be a mostly forgotten member of the Godhead whom we occasionally give a nod of recognition to, which is what He has become in most American churches. We would expect our new life with the Holy Spirit to look radically different from our old life without Him.

Yet this is not the way it is for most people. We don't live this way. For some reason, we don't think we need the Holy Spirit. We don't expect the Holy Spirit to act. Or if we do, our expectations are often misguided or self-serving. Given our talent set, experience, and education, many of us are fairly capable of living rather successfully (according to the world's standards) without any strength from the Holy Spirit.

Even our church growth can happen without Him. Let's be honest: If you combine a charismatic speaker, a talented worship band, and some hip, creative events, people will attend your church. Yet this does not mean that the Holy Spirit of God is actively working and moving in the lives of the people who are coming. It simply means that you have created a space that is appealing enough to draw people in for an hour or two on Sunday.

It certainly does not mean that people walk out the doors moved to worship and in awe of God. People are more likely to describe the quality of the music or the appeal of the sermon than the One who is the reason people gather for "church" in the first place.

I think the worst part is when you get outside the church's walls and interact with believers and nonbelievers in the same sphere. Can you really tell a difference? If you didn't recognize their faces from church, would you know from their actions and lifestyle that they were followers of Jesus? Honestly, sometimes I am embarrassed by some of my "Christian" neighbors because my unbelieving neighbors seem *more* joyful, welcoming, and at peace. Why does this happen? And how is it even possible?

Romans 8:9 says, "You, however, are not in the flesh but in the Spirit, if in fact the Spirit of God dwells in you." According to this verse, if I am a believer, the Spirit of God dwells in me. Paul reiterates that truth in 1 Corinthians 6:19–20: "Do you not know that your body is a temple of the Holy Spirit, who is in you, whom you have received from God? You are not your own; you were bought at a price" (NIV). Our bodies are the Spirit's temple. Later we will delve more into what that means for us; but essentially, it's that the Holy Spirit makes His home in our bodies. We are His place of dwelling.

And this is the question I just can't get around: If it's true that the Spirit of God dwells in us and that our bodies are the Holy Spirit's temple, then shouldn't there be a huge difference between the person who has the Spirit of God living inside of him or her and the person who does not?

This may be a silly illustration, but if I told you I had an encounter with God where He entered my body and gave me a supernatural ability to play basketball, wouldn't you expect to see an amazing improvement in my jump shot, my defense, and my speed on the court? After all, this is God we're talking about. And if you saw no change in my athleticism, wouldn't you question the validity of my "encounter"?

Churchgoers all across the nation say the Holy Spirit has entered them. They claim that God has given them a supernatural ability to follow Christ, put their sin to death, and serve the church. *Christians* talk about being *born again* and say that they were *dead* but now have come *to life*. We have become hardened to those words, but they are powerful words that have significant meaning. Yet when those outside the church see no difference in our lives, they begin to question our integrity, our sanity, or even worse, our God. And can you blame them?

It reminds me of James's frustration when he writes about freshwater springs producing saltwater. You can almost hear his incredulity as he writes, "Does a spring pour forth from the same opening both fresh and salt water?" (James 3:11). What he's saying is that so-called Christians were doing something that should've been impossible—and this kind of doing the impossible is not a good thing!

He laments, "My brothers, these things ought to not be so" (James 3:10). I echo James's exhortation to those of us in the church today: My brothers and sisters who have received the Holy Spirit, we often lack love, joy, peace, patience, kindness, etc., even while many of our unbelieving friends exhibit these traits—brothers and sisters, these things ought not to be so! Just as I advised my Jehovah's Witnesses visitors, we need to begin afresh by reexamining our preconceived ideas about the Holy Spirit and what it means to be a temple of the Spirit. There is much more to God and following in the Way of Jesus than getting a bunch of talented people together to hold a church service.

When Jesus was preparing to leave this earth, He comforted His disciples, telling them not to worry but instead to trust in Him (John 14:1). Hadn't He proven Himself faithful the past years that they had journeyed together? First, He comforted them by telling them that the separation would be only temporary and that He was going to "prepare a place" for them (14:2–3 NIV). Second, He told them that He was going to be with God the Father, and that even from there He could hear their prayers (14:12–14). Finally, Jesus gave the disciples the ultimate reassurance: Another Comforter would come. Jesus said that the Father would give the disciples "another Counselor to be with [them] forever" (14:16 NIV). In this case, the Greek word *another* means another that is just like the first (as opposed to another that is of a different sort or kind). So Jesus was saying that the One who would come would be just like Him!

Have you ever thought about the significance of having "another" Counselor who is "just like" Christ? Right now, imagine what it would be like to have Christ standing beside you in the flesh, functioning as your personal Counselor. Imagine the peace that would come from knowing you would always receive perfect truth and flawless direction from Him. That sounds amazing, and none of us could deny the benefit of having Jesus here physically, guiding and enabling us every step of the way.

Yet why do we assume that this would be any better than the literal presence of the Holy Spirit? Those of us who believe in Jesus would never deny the truth that we have the Spirit of the living God, the Spirit of Him who raised Jesus from the dead, living inside of us. I'm just not convinced we've internalized this truth and enjoyed His blessings as He intends. It seems like this is mostly head knowledge to us, and that we have not owned it. It has not really made much of a difference in our lives, to the degree that if we woke up tomorrow and discovered that it is not true the Holy Spirit lives inside of us, most likely our lives wouldn't look much different.

Jesus Himself said to His disciples, "It is for your good that I am going away. Unless I go away, the Counselor will not come to you; but if I go, I will send him to you" (John 16:7 NIV). So Jesus is basically telling His disciples, "Yes, I was with you for three and a half years, but it is better that I leave you and the Holy Spirit comes to you."

When the disciples heard that two thousand years ago, I'm sure it was hard for them to grasp. How could it be better to trade a human Jesus—a man they could talk and eat and laugh with—for a Spirit they couldn't physically see? Thousands of years later, I think most of us would also choose a physical Jesus over an invisible Spirit. But what do we do with the fact that Jesus says it is better for His followers to have the Holy Spirit? Do we believe Him? If so, do our lives reflect that belief?

My hunch is that most of you reading this book have basic knowledge *about* the Holy Spirit; but when it comes to experiencing the Spirit in your life, it's a different story. Take a moment and ask yourself this question: *When was the last time I undeniably saw the Spirit at work in or around me?* If it was recently, consider taking a few minutes to reflect on what the Spirit of God did and how you saw Him at work. Thank God for His active presence in your life, and praise Him for the way He is leading you even now.

If you are having trouble recounting a time when the Spirit was at work in or around you, perhaps that is because you have been ignoring the Spirit. Perhaps it is because you have a lot of head knowledge about the Spirit, but not much of a relationship with Him.

The reality is that the early church knew less about the Holy Spirit than most of us in the church today, at least in the intellectual sense. But they came to know the Spirit intimately and powerfully as He worked in and through their lives. All throughout the New Testament, we read of the apostles whose lives were led by the Spirit and lived out by His power.

The goal of this book is not to completely explain the Spirit or to go back to the apostolic age. The goal is to learn to live faithfully today. First of all, it is impossible for us as finite humans to completely understand an infinite God. Second, many of us don't need more knowledge about the Spirit from a cerebral vantage point—what we need is experiential knowledge of His presence. And third, we can never "go back," only forward, seeking what it means to live faithfully in the time and culture where God has placed us.

So while hopefully you will learn something new about the Holy Spirit in this book, my prayer is that it will draw you into deeper communion with the Spirit and greater experience of His power and presence in your life.

———————

Years ago, when a random thought came into my head, I decided to share it with my wife. "Have you ever wondered what caterpillars think about?" I asked.

Not surprisingly, she said, "No."

I then proceeded to tell her about the confusion I imagined a caterpillar must experience. For all its caterpillar life, it crawls around a small patch of dirt and up and down a few plants. Then one day it takes a nap. A long nap. And then, what in the world must go through its head when it wakes up to discover it can *fly?* What happened to its dirty, plump little worm body? What does it think when it sees its tiny new body and gorgeous wings?

As believers, we ought to experience this same kind of astonishment when the Holy Spirit enters our bodies. We should be stunned in disbelief over becoming a "new creation" with the Spirit living in us. As the caterpillar finds its new ability to fly, we should be thrilled over our Spirit-empowered ability to live differently and faithfully. Isn't this what the Scriptures speak of? Isn't this what we've all been longing for?

It really is an astounding truth that the Spirit of Him who raised Jesus from the dead lives in you. He lives in me. I do not know what the Spirit will do or where He'll lead me each time I invite Him to guide me. But I am tired of living in a way that looks exactly like people who do not have the Holy Spirit of God living in them. I want to consistently live with an awareness of His strength. I want to be different today from what I was yesterday as the fruit of the Spirit becomes more manifest in me.

I want to live so that I am truly submitted to the Spirit's leading on a daily basis. Christ said it is better for us that the Spirit came, and I want to live like I know that is true. I don't want to keep crawling when I have the ability to fly.

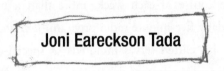

Joni Eareckson Tada

Recently I was asked, "Who is the most Spirit-filled person you know?" My response: Joni Eareckson Tada.

A 1967 diving accident left then-seventeen-year-old Joni a quadriplegic. Lying in a hospital bed, she was filled with an overwhelming desire to end her life. The thought of spending the rest of her years paralyzed from the neck down and relying on others to care for her basic needs was staggering.

But Joni did not end her life that day. Instead, she chose to surrender it to God. Little did she know that the Spirit of God would transform her into one of the godliest women ever to grace this earth. God gave her a humility and a love that enables her to look beyond her own pain and to see others' hurts. She is a person who consistently "in humility count[s] others more significant" than herself (an embodiment of Philippians 2:3).

I don't even know where to begin with all that she has done.

While undergoing two years of rehabilitation after the accident, she spent many hours learning to paint with a brush held between her teeth. Her detailed paintings and prints are now highly sought after. Her international best-selling autobiography, *Joni*, was later made into a full-length feature film. She founded Joni and Friends in 1979 to increase Christian ministry to the disabled community throughout the world. The organization led to the establishment in 2007 of the Joni and Friends International Disability Center, which currently impacts thousands of families around the globe.

Over the course of each week, more than a million people listen to her daily five-minute radio program, *Joni and Friends*. The organization she started serves hundreds of special-needs families through family retreats across the nation. Through Wheels for the World, wheelchairs are collected nationwide, refurbished by inmates in several correctional facilities, and then shipped and donated to developing nations where, whenever possible, physical therapists fit each chair to a disabled child or adult who is in need. As of 2008, Wheels for the World had cumulatively distributed 52,342 wheelchairs to 102 countries and trained hundreds of ministry and community leaders, including people with disabilities.

In 2005, Joni Eareckson Tada was appointed to the Disability Advisory Committee of the U.S. State Department. She has worked with Dr. Condoleezza Rice on programs affecting disabled persons in the State Department and around the world. Joni has appeared twice on *Larry King Live,* sharing not only her Christian testimony but a biblical perspective on right-to-life issues that affect our nation's disabled population. And on top of all that, Joni has written more than thirty-five books.

Yet it is not because of these accomplishments that I consider her the most Spirit-filled person I know. Actually, it has nothing to do with all she's accomplished. It has to do with the fact that you can't spend ten minutes with Joni before she breaks out in song, quotes Scripture, or shares a touching and timely word of encouragement. I have never seen the fruit of the Spirit more obviously displayed in a person's life as when I am with Joni. I can't seem to have a conversation with Joni without shedding tears. It's because Joni is a person whose life, at every level, gives evidence of the Spirit's work in and through her.[1]

CHAPTER 2

What Are You Afraid Of?

*The Lord challenges us to suffer persecutions and to confess
him. He wants those who belong to him to be brave and
fearless. He himself shows how weakness of the flesh is
overcome by courage of the Spirit. This is the testimony
of the apostles and in particular of the representative,
administrating Spirit. A Christian is fearless.*

-Tertullian-

Fear of rejection has paralyzed me more than once. God has answered
my prayers for greater boldness, but I would be dishonest if I did not
admit there are still times when I worry about how others view me.
Even as I write this book, I wonder how friends will respond and
how I will be labeled or even misunderstood.

Maybe caring too much about what other people think is not something you deal with personally; if so, then I am glad for it, but there is probably something else you fear. For many people, however, caring too much about what others think can be a serious, even a driving, fear.

Whole denominations have been built around specific beliefs about the Holy Spirit. I know people who have lost jobs at churches and Christian colleges because of their beliefs about the Holy Spirit. I even had a girl break up with me while I was in seminary because we believed differently about Him! It is not one of those issues that is easy to float over. This is especially true if you belong to a particular "camp" with a specific belief or bent; it is certainly natural to fear rejection from those in your camp if you change your views.

Though this fear is natural, it's not right. We are called to pattern our lives after the Way described in the Bible. We are not called to fear what following the Way of Jesus may require of us, but that doesn't mean those fears won't crop up. A life of following Christ requires relinquishing those fears when they do come. It means refusing to let your fears of what others think, your fears of rejection, keep you from pursuing the truth about the Holy Spirit and whatever else God is teaching you and calling you to.

Are you willing to pursue truth in your journey to know and be known by the Holy Spirit? Do you have enough humility to be open to the possibility that you have been wrong in your understanding of the Spirit? It's easy to get into "defensive mode," where you quickly disagree and turn to proof texts and learned arguments to defend what you've always believed. Rather than guarding your perspective, consider taking a fresh look at familiar passages to make sure you haven't missed something. You may end up with the same theology you've always had, but maybe you won't. Don't let your views be determined by a particular denomination or by what you've always been told. Within the context of relationship with other believers, seek out what God has said about His Spirit. Open up your mind and your life to the leading of the Spirit, regardless of what others may think or assume about you.

Fear has a way of channeling our thought process. Fear of stepping outside of a certain theological framework causes us to be biased in our interpretations. We work diligently to "prove" that our presuppositions were correct (another example of eisegesis) rather than simply and honestly pursuing truth.

What If God Doesn't Come Through?

Before we delve further into this conversation about the Spirit, I believe some other fears need to be identified and dealt with. One concern I've often heard (and felt) is, what if I pray for the Holy Spirit and nothing happens? What if I ask for more of the Spirit's fruit in my life and don't see any apparent "results"? It's scary to pray boldly for change or freedom from sin, because if nothing happens, then doesn't that mean God failed? Doesn't that mean His Spirit isn't all we've been told He is?

I think the fear of God failing us leads us to "cover for God." This means we ask for less, expect less, and are satisfied with less because we are afraid to ask for or expect more. We even convince ourselves that we don't *want* more—that we have all the "God" we need or could want. I can't imagine how much it pains God to see His children hold back from relationship with the Holy Spirit out of fear that He won't come through. How much it grieves Him to watch His children ignore the promises He's made throughout Scripture due to fear that those promises won't be kept! Empowering His children with the strength of the Holy Spirit is something the Father wants to do. It's not something we have to talk Him into. He genuinely wants to see us walk in His strength.

When Jesus was on earth, He said to His disciples, "If you then, who are evil, know how to give good gifts to your children, how much more will the heavenly Father give the Holy Spirit to those who ask him!" (Luke 11:13). God is a good Father who *wants* to give good gifts to His children. Sometimes I forget this truth and beg as though He needs convincing. It's as ridiculous as if my kids thought they needed to beg me to hug them. It delights my heart to hug them.

Do you believe that God in heaven gives His Spirit to those who ask? Do you *really* believe it? This truth and what it means is so incredible that no one who actually believes it could then fail to ask for the Holy Spirit.

In Acts, after Jesus has been resurrected and ascended to heaven, Peter addressed a crowd and declared, "Repent and be baptized every one of you in the name of Jesus Christ for the forgiveness of your sins, and you will receive the gift of the Holy Spirit" (2:38). We've already seen that God promises to give His Spirit to those who ask. Here we see that we receive the Holy Spirit when we begin to follow Christ.

All this leads to a question we cannot escape: Does God really give the Holy Spirit to those who ask, or was Jesus lying when He said that? I have found that it comes down to faith: Do you believe God keeps His promises or not? Do your prayers and actions give evidence of your belief?

So God has promised to give us His Spirit if we ask, if we repent and are baptized, and it comes down to whether we believe Him and act upon that promise. I realize that some of you reading this book have asked the Holy Spirit to do something and have not experienced the results you anticipated. Now you fear asking again because it would weaken your faith if God "fails to act" again. I've heard many people question God for not responding when they prayed in faith. I don't doubt that these people prayed in faith, but the question is whether they prayed for things God has promised. Often, it's the un-promised requests that God answers with a no.

There is a huge difference between believing what God has promised and praying for things you'd like to be true. I encourage you to pray confidently for what God has promised. Don't put your hope in what others promise or what you've been told you'll "get" if you are a "good Christian" (e.g., a good job, financial success, the perfect spouse, healthy children, a big house, etc.). And ultimately, you need to stake your faith in God alone, not in the gifts (good as they may be) that He gives. It really comes down to trust. Do you trust God that when He says no or "not in this way" to you, you still believe He is good and doing what is best?

Do I Even Want This?

The flip side of fearing that God won't show up is fearing that He *will*. What if God does show up but then asks you to go somewhere or do something that's uncomfortable? For many people, fearing that God will ask them to go in a difficult, undesirable direction outweighs the fear that God will ignore them.

A few years ago, I asked one of my friends if he genuinely wanted to know God's will—no matter what God desired to do through him. His answer was honest: "No, that would freak me out." He then admitted that he would rather not know everything God wants him to do. That way in the end he could say, "I had no idea You wanted me to do all of those things." I appreciate my friend's willingness to say what many secretly think and feel about total surrender to God. It's honest, more honest than most people are willing to be.

If you can relate to my friend, then at least you take God at His Word and believe the Spirit is meant to dwell in and guide our lives. When it comes down to it, many of us do not really want to be led by the Holy Spirit. Or, more fundamentally, many of us don't want to be led by anyone other than ourselves. The whole idea of giving up control (or the delusion of it) is terrifying, isn't it? Do you thrive on controlling the big and small in your life? Does the thought of letting go and listening to the Spirit's guidance scare you and only make you cling tighter to what you think you have?

The truth is that the Spirit of the living God is guaranteed to ask you to go somewhere or do something you wouldn't normally want or choose to do. The Spirit will lead you to the way of the cross, as He led Jesus to the cross, and that is definitely not a safe or pretty or comfortable place to be. The Holy Spirit of God will mold you into the person you were made to be. This often incredibly painful process strips you of selfishness, pride, and fear. For a powerful example of this, read in C. S. Lewis's book *The Voyage of the Dawn Treader* about the boy, Eustace, who becomes a dragon. In order to become a little boy again, he must undergo a tremendous amount of pain as the dragon skin is peeled away and torn from him. Only after he endures this painful process is he truly transformed from a dragon back into a boy.

Sometimes the sin we take on becomes such a part of us that it requires this same kind of ripping and tearing to free us. The Holy Spirit does not seek to hurt us, but He does seek to make us Christlike, and this can be painful.

So, if you say you want the Holy Spirit, you must first honestly ask yourself if you want to do His will. Because if you do not genuinely want to know and do His will, why should you ask for His presence at all? But if you decide you do want to know His will, there will be moments when you have to let go of the fear of what that might mean—when you have to release your grip of control on your life and decide to be led, come what may.

Is My Reputation in the Way?

I live in Southern California, where people care more about appearances than most of the rest of the United States combined. If you've lived in or even visited SoCal, you know exactly what I mean. Southern California is the land of tanning beds, plastic surgeons, designer boutiques, three-hundred-dollar jeans, nail salons, expensive real estate, excessive shopping, and hot cars. I could keep going, but I won't. It is obvious that Southern Californians care a lot about their appearances.

While this preoccupation with appearance has been taken to extremes in SoCal, it is an issue that almost every American deals with. We care a lot about what other people think of us. Maybe in Texas or Oklahoma it's about what kind of football fan you are. In Colorado, it might be how outdoorsy you seem. And maybe in New England it is which college your children attend. Obviously, these are just silly stereotypes, but the point is that we Americans tend to care about what others think of us—to an unhealthy degree. And believers certainly are not exempt from this trend.

In much the same way, many believers care too much about appearances. Even those who move past the superficial and materialistic are often very concerned with their reputation in "spiritual matters." For example, if a friend sees you reading this book about the Holy Spirit, do you worry he or she will think you too "charismatic" or "radical"? If you share about the Holy Spirit's movement in your life, do you wonder what others will think about you? Are you afraid of getting "too much" of the Holy Spirit and the possible ramifications of that? (Heaven forbid you gain a reputation for being weird or immoderate!)

Or maybe you come from a background that would consider this book too conservative. Maybe some of the biblical boundaries I've outlined are ones that people in your church label "restrictive" for a Spirit-led person.

Regardless of your background, are you willing to set it aside and just respond to biblical truth? One question I've had to ask myself repeatedly is am I even *open* to the possibility that I could be wrong in my beliefs? If so, would I have the courage to change my actions if I were shown that my interpretation of Scripture was faulty? At this point, we're all tempted to quickly respond with an "of course!" We want to believe that we are people who desire TRUTH even over relationship and acceptance. But the chances are that you care about people's opinions more than you're willing to admit.

Personally, I was raised in a very conservative church that almost totally ignored the Spirit's activity and presence in daily life. I was warned that I wouldn't feel a thing when the Holy Spirit came into me, and a hesitancy toward "taking things too far" in anything relating to the Spirit was deeply instilled in my thoughts and attitudes. After all, I didn't want to become like "them"—those people down the street who were hyped on emotions and ignored the Scriptures. I have met a lot of people with backgrounds like mine, and I've seen much damage done by choices made out of fear rather than truth. In short, we've kept the Spirit from breaking into our lives because of the fear of resembling "them."

And then there is the other side, where individuals are sometimes unwilling to listen to the warnings or checks of those "stiff and lifeless" conservatives. Perhaps you're so afraid people will think you are stifling the Holy Spirit that you won't consider examining your way of doing things—even when the Bible gives clear instructions to the contrary. Maybe you think that most conservatives are afraid of the Holy Spirit, and you fear becoming like "them."

Wherever we are at in this continuum, the point is that we need to base our understanding of and experience with the Holy Spirit on biblical truth and not on fear.

As disciples of Jesus, being in relationship with Him must be our focus. When we allow others' perceptions of us (or even our perceptions of their perceptions!) to control how we live, we are enslaved. We become entrenched in the ways of this world and do not live as citizens of heaven, which is another kind of kingdom altogether. Though there is a sense in which this kingdom of God is still future (Zech. 14:9; Acts 1:6–7), there is also a sense in which it is here now (Matt. 6:10; 12:28). As citizens of this kingdom, we are called to live in a way that reflects the reality of the kingdom of God. When we become overly concerned about our appearance, our spiritual reputation, our coolness, and our acceptance, we are living as citizens of this world rather than as ambassadors.

This is not something that just goes away. It is an ever-present struggle to maintain your true allegiance. And that is really what it comes down to: Where does your allegiance lie? Do you care about what people think when they see you, or do you care about seeking the truth concerning the Spirit of God and then living in light of the truth, holding to those promises, and enjoying that relationship?

Good Fear (or At Least Legitimate Concerns)

Having said all this, I actually think there is a legitimate kind of fear. Maybe *fear* is not the best word to describe what I am talking about. Perhaps it would be better to call it an area that we need to check ourselves in.

I am talking about quenching the Holy Spirit. As I said earlier, I think that quite often we worry a lot more about how people will respond to us than we do about how the Holy Spirit of God will respond. We think about making our friends mad or not being accepted or being thought of as different or strange. But rarely (if ever) do we consider whether our actions or lifestyle are grievous to the Spirit of the living God. When we put it that way, it seems more than a little ludicrous!

You're probably familiar with God's command in 1 Thessalonians 5:19, "Do not quench the Spirit." Are you concerned about breaking this command? Do you know what it means to quench the Spirit? For years I never gave it much thought. I didn't take the time to explore what this meant and how I could be guilty of this sin. Like most people, I just assumed I wasn't quenching the Spirit, and I moved on.

I look back now and realize I not only quenched the Spirit, but I also violated the next verse: "Do not treat prophecies with contempt" (1 Thess. 5:20 NIV). I had contempt toward anyone who claimed to have "a word from the Lord." I felt it was a righteous contempt because I'd seen people use the phrase "I have a word from the Lord" to manipulate others for personal gain. Cult leaders use the phrase to secure followers and increase their own authority. How can you disagree or even have a discussion with someone who claims they heard directly from God?

So I was against all of it. I was disturbed by any claim of prophetic speech. Looking back, I believe my concerns were valid but my actions were not. The biblical response would have been to "test everything. Hold on to the good. Avoid every kind of evil" (1 Thess. 5:21–22 NIV). Rather than rejecting the possibility of God supernaturally speaking through people, I should have tested what I was hearing in the context of faithful community.

Another valid test for prophecy is the standard of edification. The purpose of prophecy is to encourage and build up the body of Christ. Like every other gift, if it is not done out of love, it is meaningless (1 Cor. 13:2, 8; 14:3, 31). This is a good antidote to my previous inclination to ignore all prophetic speech. In doing that I was hindering the work of the Spirit, and I do not want to do so again.

On the flip side, if churches that practice prophetic utterances were quicker to reject the false prophets and prophecies by calling them out on their biblical inconsistencies ("avoiding evil"), then maybe the conservative world would be less skeptical about prophecy. If there was in place a healthy system of communal accountability and a commitment to biblical integrity, then maybe we would be slower to quench the Spirit in this regard. We would be quicker to "hold on to the good" instead of throwing out the good and the bad in one fell swoop.

Another important check is going too far with all this. No, I am not contradicting what I wrote previously. I don't mean "going too far" in the sense of getting too radical or passionate about the Holy Spirit. I mean "going too far" in the sense of stepping outside the bounds of biblical orthodoxy. I mean "going too far" in the sense of adding to the Scriptures or listening to distortions of the truth, supposedly from the Holy Spirit, and applying those to your life. This is why orthodox (as in "committed to exegetical living") and radical (as in "willing to do whatever and go wherever the Spirit leads, even if it doesn't make sense") community is vital to living lives that comply with the leading of the Holy Spirit.

Some conservatives may quench the Spirit by ignoring His working, but surely putting unbiblical words into the mouth of God is a form of quenching the Spirit as well. We need the Spirit in order to live faithfully. But we also need one another as we work out our faith.

Take some time to consider what fears you have about the Holy Spirit. It may take a while to pinpoint exactly what your attitudes and responses toward the Holy Spirit have been. Don't hide your fears. Admit them, first to yourself, and then to God (who knows all of them already yet desires to have us share our fears with Him). As you come to Him, be honest about how you fear disappointing people more than quenching His Spirit, or how you don't really trust Him to come through on His promises, or whatever else you may be feeling toward Him.

Finally, share this with people you trust, people you can have these sorts of conversations with. Allow the Spirit to continue His work of freeing you from unnecessary fear and inhibition or from unrestricted license. Surrender yourself and invite Him truly to dwell within you, whatever that may mean and wherever it may take you.

I know that by writing a book about the Holy Spirit, I will be labeled. The irony is that I don't even know how to label myself. I was saved in a Baptist church, attended a charismatic Bible study, went to a conservative seminary while working at seeker-driven churches, partnered with Pentecostal movements, and have spoken at a wide variety of denominational conferences.

I'm not even sure how to label my current church. All I know is that we definitely believe in the Holy Spirit and hope to experience more of Him every minute. When you get down to it, is there anything else we really need to know? Do we need to label one another "conservative" or "charismatic" or "radical"? What's the point in that? Let's focus on believing the promises given to us by God, on submitting to Him the fears that we have, and on surrendering ourselves fully to the work and will of God, the Holy Spirit.

Domingo and Irene Garcia

He's a mechanic. She's a hairdresser. They have been foster parents to thirty-two children and have adopted sixteen. Domingo and Irene are in their late fifties and currently have eleven children living with them, and they tell me they would take more if they could. Anyone who has children knows they could be doing this only by the Spirit's power. Imagine the amount of love, joy, peace, patience, kindness, goodness, faithfulness, gentleness, and self-control it would take to pull this off.

Domingo and Irene take the command in James 1:27 (caring for orphans) more seriously than any other Americans I know. While other people their age are figuring out how to live most comfortably, they can't stop thinking of the 500,000 kids in America who need parents. And while they see these kids as a huge blessing, they are also very open about the hardships they face daily. Perseverance has been key, especially years ago when one of their adopted sons hung himself in their closet. While their days are filled with joy, there have also been many times when they persevered by sheer obedience.

God has provided for them over and over again. One time they needed to build an addition onto their house so that they could take in more children. They didn't have the money, so Irene prayed fervently. When she looked up from praying, the first thing she saw was a sign for a contractor. She immediately asked God, "Is he the answer to my prayer?" Days later, one of the leaders in their church heard about their need and offered to build the addition for free. And you guessed it—he was the same contractor whose name Irene had seen on the sign.

One of the wonderful blessings they have enjoyed is watching their biological children follow in their footsteps. One of their sons has two biological and two adopted kids. Another son has three biological and three adopted kids. They live such extraordinary lives that CBS news ran a story on them. Even the secular world notices the unusual and supernatural love these two have shown to those in need.

For those who may think that Domingo and Irene have always been as gracious as they are today, let me share some insight from their past (I have permission). Irene has shared publicly about the early days in their marriage and the hatred she felt toward Domingo. He was abusive, and she prayed regularly that he would die. She even daydreamed about him driving off a cliff because of the pain he inflicted on her. Now she calls him the godliest man she knows.

For anyone who thinks their own life or marriage is hopeless, remember Domingo and Irene. God loves to take people in the worst of situations and transform them by His Spirit.

CHAPTER 3

Theology of the Holy Spirit 101

What does the Spirit do? His works are ineffable in
majesty, and innumerable in quantity. How can we
even ponder what extends beyond the ages? What did
He do before creation began? How great are the graces
He showered on creation? What power will He wield
in the age to come? He existed; He pre-existed; He co-
existed with the Father and the Son before the ages.
Even if you can imagine anything beyond the ages, you
will discover that the Spirit is even further beyond.

-St. Basil the Great-

Perhaps you wonder why I am talking about the theology of the
Holy Spirit in this chapter. Aren't the most important aspects of life

what you *do* and how you *live?* Does it really matter what you *think* about something?

These are legitimate questions.

What you do and how you live are absolutely vital. Without action and fruit, all the theology in the world has little meaning. But theology is still important—what you believe absolutely determines how you act. So while good theology at its best can lead us to live godly lives, bad theology will always point us in the wrong direction. When we study the Holy Spirit, bad theology can lead to ineffective lives or, worse yet, lives spent striving after what the Spirit of God opposes. So in this chapter we will ground our understanding of the Holy Spirit by looking at some basic biblical statements about who He is and what He does.

When I was in seminary, I discovered a lot of scholars far more intelligent than I, many of whom spent years studying particular aspects of theology. I frequently read articles by brilliant individuals who expressed opposing views on various issues, and it was hard to decide what I really believed was right. Each side would have convincing arguments and well-made points (as I said, they were brilliant). When I would finish my study of one of these issues, I typically came away with a general bent toward a particular side but could rarely say I was sure beyond the shadow of a doubt. And I never made peace with the statement one professor made: "If you're fifty-one percent sure, preach it like you're one hundred percent." How is that not deception? If I'm only 90 percent sure, why not just say so?

While some of the debates and conversations that take place are peripheral and don't have to be definitively resolved in order for us to live a faithful life, many theological issues are not this way. Some theological issues are absolutely vital to our faith. These are the ones where what we believe determines how we act.

When it comes to the doctrine of the Holy Spirit, I don't want to get caught up in abstract and nebulous distinctions. I want to focus on the theological issues that shape our faith and behavior.

As I thought about this chapter, I realized how ludicrous it would be for *anyone* to say they were going to explain the Holy Spirit. The Bible says we cannot fully understand God, and I am certainly not the exception to that rule. There are things about God that are mysterious and secret, things we will never know about Him. But there also are things revealed, and those belong to us (Deut. 29:29).

In this chapter I am going to talk about some of the things that have been revealed about the Holy Spirit. I will talk about what He does in our lives and in the world and about what He is like. Keep in mind this is not an exhaustive study of the Holy Spirit. I will not cover every verse in the Bible that references the Holy Spirit because even if I did, the Spirit is infinite and cannot be known fully by humans.

Know that even as you seek to understand the Spirit more, He is so much more and bigger than you will ever be able to grasp. This is not an excuse to stop seeking to know Him, but don't limit Him to what you can learn about Him. The point is not to completely understand God but to worship Him. Let the very fact that you *cannot* know Him fully lead you to praise Him for His infiniteness and grandeur.

As we approach this conversation, let us not forget that we tread on holy ground. The Holy Spirit brought creation to life and continues to sustain it. As we read in the book of Job, "The Spirit of God has made me; the breath of the Almighty gives me life" (33:4 NIV). I can keep writing only because He allows me to. You can keep reading only because He empowers and sustains you.

I have heard the Father, Son, and Holy Spirit described like the three parts of an egg: the shell, the white stuff, and the yolk. I have also heard people say that God is like a three-leaf clover: three "arms," yet all are a part of the one clover stalk. Another popular comparison is to the three forms of H_2O (water, ice, and steam).

While these serve as cute metaphors for an unexplainable mystery, the fact is that God is not *like* an egg, a three-leaf clover, or the three forms of water. God is not *like* anything. He is incomprehensible, incomparable, and unlike any other being. He is outside our realm of existence and, thus, outside our ability to categorize Him. While analogies may be helpful in understanding certain aspects of Him, let's be careful not to think that our analogies in any way encapsulate His nature.

I love the verse in Isaiah that is typically seen as a Christmastime verse. It reads, "For to us a child is born, to us a son is given; and the government shall be upon his shoulder, and his name shall be called Wonderful Counselor, Mighty God, Everlasting Father, Prince of Peace" (9:6). Right there in that oft-quoted verse we see the Son referred to as the "Counselor" and the "Father"! This passage (and many others) keeps us from oversimplifying a divine mystery. It is not easily broken down into three main points that just make sense, but it works. And it is beautiful. The Father, the Son, and the Holy Spirit are One.

As we begin studying basic truths of the Holy Spirit, we could begin as far back as Genesis, where we see that the Spirit was present and active in creation, and then trace His actions through the whole of the Old Testament. But we will start our overview in the book of Acts, when the Spirit descended and began to indwell the disciples. The first two verses in chapter 2 say that "they were all together in one place," and that all of a sudden, a sound came from heaven that was like "a mighty rushing wind." The text says it "filled the entire house where they were sitting."

Imagine this scene with me. Jesus Christ, the one you have spent the last three years following, the one you have dedicated your life to, just ascended to heaven. You saw it with your own eyes. You and the people who have become as close as your own family are all gathered in Jerusalem in someone's house, waiting. You know that something is coming because Jesus told you about it. He said to wait, but you don't know exactly what (or in this case, who) you are waiting for. Maybe you are getting tired of wondering how many more days before something (what, you have no idea) happens.

Suddenly, a sound fills the whole house. And then tongues of fire appear and come to rest on each person present. And then it happens. Verse four reads, "And they were all filled with the Holy Spirit."

Now these are the same disciples who were dedicated to following Jesus no matter what, but who scattered as soon as Jesus was arrested.

And here they were gathered together, no doubt confused about how they should proceed now that Jesus had ascended. Yet when the Holy Spirit descended and indwelt them, a radical change occurred. From that point on, none of these disciples was ever the same. The book of Acts is a testament to this fact. We read of Stephen, the first martyr. We see Peter, a changed, courageous man. We see Paul (formerly Saul) go from killing Christ followers to becoming one and showing many others how to do so too. They were no longer timid or confused; they were bold and inspired and began to declare and live the gospel of Jesus through the power of the Holy Spirit. Think about what a huge moment this was in the lives of the disciples.

A multitude of people had gathered. Peter preached a powerful sermon, and when they heard his words, they were "cut to the heart" and asked how they should respond. Peter answered, "Repent and be baptized every one of you in the name of Jesus Christ for the forgiveness of your sins, and you will receive the gift of the Holy Spirit. For the promise is for you and for your children and for all who are far off, everyone whom the Lord our God calls to himself" (Acts 2:38–39). The text says that on that day around three thousand people became part of God's kingdom and accepted the gift of the Holy Spirit.

I think it's needless for us to debate about when the Holy Spirit becomes a part of someone's life. In my own life, was it when I first prayed as a little kid and believed I was speaking to Someone? Was it in junior high, when I raised my hand after hearing an evangelist who literally scared the hell out of me? Was it when I got baptized? Was it in high school, when I actually had a personal relationship with Jesus? Could it have been in college, when I came forward at a charismatic Bible study to "receive the Spirit"? Or was it later in life, when I chose to surrender my life fully to Jesus?

We can easily fall into the trap of fixating on these questions and miss the crux of Peter's message. When I was preaching through this passage at my church, my seven-year-old daughter, Mercy, understood. She came to me afterward and said, "Dad, I want to repent of my sins and be baptized and receive the gift of the Holy Spirit." I loved the simplicity and greatness of her faith. She didn't need to debate the finer points of how and when, exactly, the Holy Spirit would come. She just wanted to obey the passage to the best of her ability. I realize Mercy doesn't have the biblical knowledge many of us do, but I wonder how many of us have the faith she has.

Is that your response to the Word? Is it clear to you that you're supposed to repent, be baptized, and receive the Holy Spirit? If so, have you done it? If not, what keeps you from doing it today?

Why do we sometimes feel that we need to debate this endlessly, running through every possible hypothetical situation and answering every theological question first? When will we simply respond to the truth we have heard and then work through our questions from there?

——————

Now that we have a context for how the Spirit came to the first disciples and what we are told to do in response, we will shift the focus to some practical truths about who the Spirit is and what He does in our lives.

First, **the Holy Spirit is a Person.** He is not an indistinct "power" or "thing." I often hear people refer to the Spirit as an "it," as if the Spirit is a thing or force that we can control or use. This distinction may seem subtle or trivial, but it is actually a very serious misunderstanding of the Spirit and His role in our lives. In John 14:17, we read that the Spirit "dwells with you and will be in you." This calls us to relationship with the Spirit, instead of allowing us to think we can treat the Spirit as a power to be harnessed in order to accomplish our own purposes. The Holy Spirit is a Person who has personal relationships with not only believers, as we have seen, but also with the Father and the Son. We see the Spirit working in conjunction with the Father and the Son multiple times throughout the Scriptures (Matt. 28:19; 2 Cor. 13:14).

Second, **the Holy Spirit is God**. He is not a lesser or different kind of Being than God the Father or God the Son. The Spirit is God. The words *Spirit* and *God* are used interchangeably in the New Testament. In Acts we read of Peter's challenge to Ananias: "How is it that Satan has so filled your heart that you have lied to the Holy Spirit and have kept for yourself some of the money you received for the land? ... What made you think of doing such a thing? You have not lied just to human beings but to God" (5:3–4 TNIV). In these verses we see that Peter explicitly refers to the Holy Spirit as God. This is vital to remember. When we forget about the Spirit, we really are forgetting God.

Third, **the Holy Spirit is eternal and holy.** We read in the gospel of John about Jesus' promise to His disciples that the Spirit will be with them forever (14:16). And in Hebrews we read that it was through "the eternal Spirit" that Jesus "offered himself unblemished to God" (9:14 NIV). The Spirit is not just a flighty, whimsical spirit who comes and goes like the wind. He is an eternal being. The Spirit is also holy. Obviously, we commonly call Him the "Holy Spirit," and this is reinforced throughout the New Testament (Romans 1:4 and 5:5 are two examples). But consider this truly amazing fact: Because the Spirit is holy and dwells in us, our bodies are holy sanctuaries from God's vantage point. Too often we disdain our bodies as the source of sin and our fallenness; yet they are precisely where God the Spirit chooses to dwell!

Fourth, **the Holy Spirit has His own mind, and He prays for us**. Romans 8:27 says, "He who searches hearts knows what is the mind of the Spirit, because the Spirit intercedes for the saints according to the will of God." I don't know about you, but I find the thought of the Spirit of God praying for me according to the will of God extremely comforting.

So many times in life I haven't known what to pray, either for myself or for others. Other times I pray for stupid things.

For example, a while back I was out golfing with some friends and decided I really wanted to shoot in the 70s (I generally am in the 90s). So in a moment of shallowness, I prayed that God would empower me to play my best round ever. I guess the Holy Spirit was praying too, because that day I shot 115 (possibly my worst score ever). The Spirit knew I needed to work on my anger and humility, instead of adding to my pride.

In any given situation, we may not know exactly how we should pray or what we should do. But we can take confidence in the fact that the Holy Spirit knows our hearts and the will of God, and He is always interceding on our behalf.

Fifth, **the Spirit has emotions**. For a long time, whenever I read that we are not to grieve the Holy Spirit (Isa. 63:10; Eph. 4:30), I thought that was a bit of an exaggeration. It almost seems sacrilegious to say that I could grieve God. Who am I to have such power over the Spirit? That doesn't seem right. In fact, it even seemed wrong to say that God has feelings; for some reason I felt it belittled Him.

I struggled with these thoughts for a while until I finally realized where they were coming from. In our culture, having feelings or emotions is equated with weakness. This is a lie that is deeply ingrained in many of us.

God created feelings. Sure, like anything else, they can be misused and abused. But the intent and purpose of feelings came from God. Since He created emotions, why is it difficult to believe that He Himself has emotions? The Spirit is grieved when there is a breach in relationship, whether it be relationship with God or relationship with other people. When we are disunified, unloving, hateful, jealous, gossipy, etc., that is when we grieve the Spirit of God. And since He is the creator of emotions, I believe that the Spirit grieves more deeply than we can even understand.

How do you respond when you hear this? Does it bother you? When was the last time you were saddened because your sin pained the Holy Spirit?

A while back, two women from my church grew increasingly angry at each other. The three of us sat in my office, and I listened to them passionately express the reasons for their frustration. I lacked the wisdom to determine who was "more in the wrong." I just wept as they spoke. I told them I was deeply saddened because I knew how much our Father hated this. While it is rare that I'm brought to tears, there have been numerous times when I am burdened by the grief that members of Cornerstone Church have heaped upon the Holy Spirit through stubbornness and lack of forgiveness.

I believe that if we truly cared about the Holy Spirit's grief, there would be fewer fights, divorces, and splits in our churches. Maybe it's not due to a lack of belief but rather a lack of concern. I pray for the day when believers care more about the Spirit's grief than their own. In fact, I pray that some of you readers would be broken over the grief you've placed on the Holy Spirit. So broken that you actually put down this book and work to resolve any conflicts you have with other believers.

"If possible, so far as it depends on you, live peaceably with all" (Rom. 12:18).

Sixth, **the Holy Spirit has His own desires and will**. In 1 Corinthians we read that the gifts of the Spirit are "empowered by one and the same Spirit, who apportions to each one individually as he wills" (12:11). This is an important reminder of *who* is in control. Just as we don't get to choose which gifts we are given, so also we don't get to choose what God intends for us or for the church. The Spirit has a plan for our lives, for each of us. And He has a plan for the church, including your individual church body and the worldwide body of Christ.

If you are like me, you probably have a plan for your own life, for your church, and maybe even for the larger body of Christ. That's why we all desperately need to pray, as Christ did, "Not my will, but yours be done."

Seventh, **the Holy Spirit is omnipotent, omnipresent, and omniscient.** These are theological words that essentially mean that the

Spirit is all-powerful (e.g., Zech. 4:6), present everywhere (e.g., Ps. 139:7–8), and all-knowing (e.g., 1 Cor. 2:10b), respectively. These are some of His attributes that we will never fully grasp as finite human beings. In Isaiah we read, "Who can fathom the Spirit of the LORD, or instruct the LORD as his counselor?" (40:13 TNIV). Though we will never be able to perfectly articulate or completely understand these attributes, may these aspects of the Spirit lead us to praise, even with imperfect words and incomplete understanding!

If the Holy Spirit dwells within you, a number of things should be a part of your life. I am going to explore several, but don't allow yourself just to read through these items like a grocery-store list. If you merely skim this list, you'll miss out on my favorite part of this book. I have benefited so much from taking each of these promises literally, meditating on them, and asking for them. Take time to dwell on each one. Consider how each one is manifest in your life; and if it isn't, spend some time asking God for that specific thing.

- The Spirit helps us speak when we are in precarious situations and need to bear witness (Mark 13:11; Luke 12:12).

- The Counselor teaches and reminds us of what we need to know and remember. He is our comforter, our advisor, our encourager, and our strength. He guides us in the way we should go (Ps. 143:10;

John 14–16; Acts 9:31; 13:2; 15:28; 1 Cor. 2:9–10; 1 John 5:6–8).

- From the Spirit we receive power to be God's witnesses to the ends of the earth. It is the Spirit who draws people to the gospel, the Spirit who equips us with the strength we need to accomplish God's purposes. The Holy Spirit not only initially draws people to God, He also draws believers closer to Jesus (Acts 1:8; Rom. 8:26; Eph. 3:16–19).

- By the power of the Spirit we put to death the misdeeds of the body. The Spirit sets us free from the sins we cannot get rid of on our own. This is a lifelong process we entered into, in partnership with the Spirit, when we first believed (e.g., Rom. 8:2).

- Through the Spirit we have received a spirit of adoption as children, which leads us into intimacy with the Father, instead of a relationship based on fear and slavery. The Spirit bears witness to us that we are His children (Rom. 8:15–16).

- The Holy Spirit convicts people of sin. He does this both before we initially enter into right relationship with God and as we journey through this life as believers (John 16:7–11; 1 Thess. 1:5).

- The Spirit brings us life and freedom. Where the Spirit is, there is freedom, not bondage or slavery. In our world that is plagued with death, this is a profound truth that points to real hope (Rom. 8:10–11; 2 Cor. 3:17).

- By the power of the Holy Spirit we abound with hope because our God is a God of hope, who fills His children with all joy and peace (Rom. 15:13).

- As members of God's kingdom community, each of us is given a manifestation of the Spirit in our lives for the purpose of the common good. We all have something to offer because of what the Spirit gives to us (1 Cor. 12:7).

- The fruit of being led by the Spirit of God includes love, joy, peace, patience, kindness, goodness, faithfulness, gentleness, and self-control. These attitudes and actions will characterize our lives as we allow ourselves to be grown and molded by the Spirit. The Spirit is our sanctifier (2 Cor. 3:18; Gal. 5:22–23).

My hope is that reading these truths about the Holy Spirit will lead you into a deeper relationship with and a greater reverence for the

Spirit—that good theology would lead you to right action, genuine love, and true worship.

Perhaps you read these verses and wonder why these things are not a part of your life. Don't be discouraged. Ask God to make you more loving or to help you put to death the deeds of the flesh or to use you to bless His children. Remember that we cannot do these things on our own, and that these are the very things the Holy Spirit does in our lives. The Father tells us to ask Him. And we can ask confidently because we are asking for things God promises us in the Bible. May we grow in relationship with the Spirit more and more, and belittle and ignore Him less and less.

Francis Schaeffer

Francis Schaeffer was an American who was born in 1912 and died in 1984. During the course of his life he had a profound effect on Christian thought and culture. Some have even said that other than C. S. Lewis, no one helped shaped popular Christian thinking in the twentieth century more than Schaeffer did.

A onetime agnostic, Schaeffer eventually became a Presbyterian minister and an effective apologist and theologian for the faith. He recognized that Christianity and the Bible spoke to the big questions raised by philosophy, but that very little dialogue was happening between theologians and philosophers. So he began initiating such dialogue.

Francis and his wife, Edith, moved to Switzerland after World War II ended. Once there, they followed God's leading and in faith opened their home as a place where people with questions could come seeking answers. The stories of the ways they trusted God, both financially and practically, are absolutely inspiring. When they had a need, they would simply pray earnestly, often in prayer rotations through the night, until God provided.

The Schaeffers believed that Christianity speaks to every aspect of life, and this meant that honest questions were always welcome. Inasmuch as they sought God with their minds, the Schaeffers sought to live out their faith in community in a daily way. God's hand was distinctively guiding them to establish what would come to be called *L'Abri,* the French word for "shelter." It was so named by the Schaeffers because many people came there to ask honest questions about God and life's meaning in a safe place. It is still active at its original location in Switzerland, and there are several other centers around the world.

In conversations with the thousands of students and travelers who came to L'Abri (some staying a night, some months, and some years) from all kinds of backgrounds and religions, Francis always communicated that through the Bible humans can know the "true truth" about God and themselves. In addition to engaging those who came to L'Abri, Francis also wrote numerous books, lectured at universities, and spoke in several countries.

He truly loved God with all his heart and with all his mind, and thousands of lives have been (and continue to be) touched because of it. This is what happens when a person submits to the Spirit and allows Him to have *His* way in life.[2]

CHAPTER 4

Why Do You Want Him?

The Christian's life in all its aspects—intellectual and ethical, devotional and relational, upsurging in worship and outgoing in witness—is supernatural; only the Spirit can initiate and sustain it. So apart from him, not only will there be no lively believers and no lively congregations, there will be no believers and no congregations at all.

-J. I. Packer-

My guess is that you would love to be filled with supernatural power from the Holy Spirit. You probably wouldn't be reading this book if you didn't. The question I want to ask is why?

Recently, a man dying of cancer asked the church elders to anoint him with oil and pray for his healing. Before we prayed, however, I asked the man a question I don't normally ask: "Why do you want to be healed? Why do you want to stay on this earth?" The man, as well as everyone else around, seemed a bit surprised that I would ask such a blunt question.

The reason I probed like this is because in the epistle of James, we are reminded that we often don't receive the answers to our prayers because we ask for the wrong reasons: "You ask and do not receive, because you ask wrongly, to spend it on your passions" (James 4:3). Our desire to live should be for the sake and glory of the God who put us on this earth in the first place.

So, really, why do you desire the Holy Spirit's activity in your life? Do you want to experience more of the Holy Spirit merely for your own benefit? When the answer is yes, then we are no different from Simon the magician, who tried to buy the Holy Spirit's power from the apostles. Peter's response to Simon in that situation was strong; he said, "May your silver perish with you, because you thought you could obtain the gift of God with money!" (Acts 8:20).

The Holy Spirit is not a commodity to be bought or traded according to our individual wants, whims, or even our felt needs. We absolutely cannot have this discussion about the Holy Spirit without calling our motives into question.

Right now I want you to take a break from reading and spend some time asking yourself *why* you want the Holy Spirit. Is it for power? Is it for your own betterment and purposes? Or is it because you want to experience all that God has for you? Is it because you love the church and desire to be a better servant to your sisters and brothers?

The Right Reason

While we may have our own purposes for desiring the Spirit's presence and power in our lives, so does God! First Corinthians 12 tells us that each follower of Christ is given a "manifestation of the Spirit for the *common good*" (v. 7). As we've seen, these manifestations, or gifts, are "empowered by one and the same Spirit, who apportions to each one individually as he wills" (v. 11).

So these reflections of the Spirit's presence and activity in us have nothing to do with our natural abilities, and we have not received them because we have earned or somehow deserve them. Since these gifts come according to God's will and not ours, it should be clear that they should not be used for our own boasting or entertainment.

The Spirit is intentional as He apportions these spiritual gifts to each person, according to His will and purposes. The most obvious and stated purpose of these manifestations is for the good and edification of the church. The Spirit desires to use us when our hearts are aligned with this vision, when we are filled with genuine love for the church, and when we desire to see the church grow in love for God and others.

On a scale of one to ten, how much do you love the church? As you look around at your brothers and sisters, do you think to yourself, *I love these people so much. I pray God empowers me in some way to encourage these people toward a deeper walk with Him*?

How much do you care? The Holy Spirit has given you a supernatural ability to serve the people God has placed around you. If God cares enough about His church to give you this Spirit-empowered ability, shouldn't you care enough about the church to use that gift for the same purpose?

The apostle Paul wanted desperately to go to heaven, but he was torn because he loved the church so much. His love for the church was the only thing that kept him tied to life on earth. He wrote, "I am hard pressed between the two. My desire is to depart and be with Christ, for that is far better. But to remain in the flesh is more necessary on your account. Convinced of this, I know that I will remain and continue with you all, for your progress and joy in the faith" (Phil. 1:23–25).

Do you resonate with Paul's purpose in life and love for the church? There are far too many people who seek the Spirit for the wrong reasons.

Attention

The Holy Spirit works to glorify Christ (John 16:14), yet so many who emphasize the Holy Spirit seem to draw attention to themselves. The Corinthian church was notorious for this. The church became chaotic because individuals were not concerned with the betterment of the church. They were trying to use manifestations of the Spirit for their own glory. They weren't interested in what God was doing in others; they just wanted to show off what God was doing in them. As they all fought for attention, it resulted in mass confusion as everyone tried to speak at the same time (1 Cor. 14:23–33).

A sure sign of the Holy Spirit's working is that Christ is magnified, not people. Self-glorification is something many of us struggle with. While my pride is still a struggle, God has been teaching me to see things from His perspective.

As a younger man, much of me craved God's power in my life because I wanted the attention. Now I want God's power because I don't want the attention. Jesus says in Matthew 5:16, "In the same way, let your light shine before others, so that they may see your good works and give glory to your Father who is in heaven." It is possible for us to be doing incredible things for the kingdom yet have people give glory to God rather than to us. Has this ever happened to you? Or do people praise you for your good works?

When the Holy Spirit truly moves, God is the one praised. Jesus is the one lifted up. When the Spirit moved at Pentecost, people knew there was a power present that came from God. That's why they didn't leave saying, "John is amazing! He learned a new language in a matter of seconds!" They knew it had to be God. Let's pray that God would empower us so radically that we would get no glory. That people would see our works and glorify God.

"So with yourselves, since you are eager for manifestations of the Spirit, strive to excel in building up the church" (1 Cor. 14:12).

Miracle Hunting

It is truly awesome (I try not to overuse that term, but believe it fits here) when a miracle takes place—when you experience something that couldn't happen by natural means. I have yet to meet someone who wouldn't want to see a miracle. My concern is that I've met many people whose pursuit of miracles is greater than their pursuit of God.

A lot of people want to talk about supernatural things like miracles, healing, or prophecy. But focusing inordinately on these things quickly becomes misguided. God calls us to pursue Him, not what He might do for us or even in our midst. Scripture emphasizes that we should desire fruit, that we should concern ourselves with becoming more like His Son. God wants us to seek to listen to His Spirit and to obey. The point of it all was never the miracles in and of themselves. Those came when they were unexpected, when people were faithful and focused on serving and loving others.

God wants us to trust Him to provide miracles when He sees fit. He doesn't just dole them out mechanically, as if we can put in a quarter, pray the right prayer, and out comes a miracle. Miracles are never an end in themselves; they are always a means to point to and accomplish something greater.

I'd love to witness more miracles. But when we make miracles the focus of our energy and pursuit, we ignore the priorities God tells us to pursue and we impose our own desires upon God. Sometimes we even resemble Satan, who told Jesus to jump off of the temple and perform a miracle. Of course God the Father could have saved Jesus from harm had He jumped, but Jesus refused to test His Father (Matt. 4:7) by "making" Him perform a miracle.

———

God does miracles when He sees fit and for His own purposes. We need to run from the temptation to conjure up miracles that

God never promised to give. Instead, we are called to focus on the priorities He has outlined for us in Scripture and ask the Holy Spirit to empower us *as He sees fit*. Ask Him to supernaturally enable you to love Him and others. And let's trust Him to display miracles for His glory, in His time, and in His way.

We also need to look for His action in the midst of our daily lives. For example, perhaps today if you live in Southern California it really is supernatural not to be materialistic.

It used to be that if I had a great worship experience, I asked God to duplicate it the next time I came to worship. Like the kid impressed by a silly magic trick, I would pray, "Do it again!" One thing I've learned about God over the years, however, is that He rarely "does it again." He's the Creator, which means that He is (among other things) creative. If we expect God to perform certain miracles or to give us a particular experience, it will be tempting to manipulate or even fake experiences of the supernatural. The point in all this is simply calling us to pursue Christ and grow in our obedience to Him, rather than pursuing the supernatural for its own sake.

Followers or Leaders?

There have been many times when I've tried to lead the Holy Spirit. I've wanted to direct Him and tell Him what to do and when to do it. The irony is that the Holy Spirit was given to direct us. Desiring the Holy Spirit means we allow the Holy Spirit to guide us. By definition, it's ridiculous to desire the Holy Spirit for our own purposes.

The Spirit is not a passive power that we can wield as we choose. The Spirit is God, a Being who requires that we submit ourselves to be led by

Him. Do you really want to be led? Even people who are natural leaders don't get to lead the Spirit. Everyone is called to be led by Him.

I honestly believe that most of us—while we might *say* we want to be led by the Spirit—are actually scared of this reality. I know I am. What would it mean? What if He asks you to give up something you're not ready to give up? What if He leads you where you don't want to go? What if he tells you to change jobs? To move? Are you willing to surrender to Him, no matter where He wants to take you? Am I?

The fact is that God is calling. The Spirit is beckoning. The real question is will you follow? Will you listen? I know I prefer a multiple-choice option for what God is asking me to do. That way, if I don't like A or B, there are always options C and D. Sometimes, of course, this is exactly how the Spirit leads us. There can be two equally good choices that God lets us choose between.

Many times, though, this is not how He works. In these cases, He calls us to do something, a particular thing, and we have the choice to obey or not. The truly startling thought is that by not submitting and totally trusting the Holy Spirit, I am not submitting to or trusting God. This is no small matter.

We all have to answer the question: *Do I want to lead or be led by the Spirit?*

Did God lead you to where you are? A lot of people in my church and in my travels tell me, "I believe that God has called me to Simi Valley." Or Wichita. Or New York. Or Greenville. Or wherever. That very well may be the case. But it could also be a cop-out because you like where you live. You have a good job. The school district is safe and has high ratings. Your family lives close by (or perhaps far away, depending on your relationship with them). It makes sense that you are "called" to be there, right?

And maybe you *are* called to where you live. But if you say you are called to be in the place you are, a few questions need to be considered. For example, how would you be missed if you left this place? What would change? Basically, what difference does your presence here make? Or, as my youth pastor once asked me, what would your church (and the worldwide church) look like if everyone was as committed as you are? If everyone gave and served and prayed exactly like you, would the church be healthy and empowered? Or would it be weak and listless?

My purpose in posing these questions is not to convince you to "go into the ministry." I'm not about recruiting pastors or missionaries. My purpose in these questions is to get you to take 1 Corinthians 12 seriously, to believe that *you* have been given a manifestation of the Spirit and that your church, the worldwide body of Christ, and the world are crippled without your involvement. I write this because I love the church and want you to trust that you are more than just a helpful addition. You need to believe you are a vital member. As real estate brokers, salesclerks, restaurant servers, baristas, teachers, dietitians, therapists, students, parents, farmers, school board members, and city council officials, you are vital members of the body of Christ. Ask yourself, *Do I believe the church needs me like a body needs a mouth?*

As part of the Spirit's work through us for the "common good," He empowers us to be His witnesses. If you are a teacher, have you thought about how you impact the students in your classes? If you are a coach, what sort of influence do you have on your team? What about other coaches you interact with? If you are a businessperson, how do you conduct yourself toward your customers and coworkers? Do they see a person who lives according to the Way of Jesus or someone who does business according to capitalistic and self-centered standards, just like everyone else? If you are a stay-at-home mom, how are you forming your children into lovers of Jesus? How are you reaching out and ministering to the neighbors God has placed around you?

It is true that God may have called you to be exactly where you are. But it's absolutely vital to grasp that He didn't call you there so you could settle in and live out your life in comfort and superficial peace. His purposes are not random or arbitrary. If you are still alive on this planet, it's because He has something for you to do. He placed us on this earth for purposes that He orchestrated long before we were born (Eph. 2:8–10). Do you believe you exist not for your own pleasure but to help people know the love of Jesus and to come fully alive in Him? If so, then that will shape how you live your life in the place where you are.

When the Spirit Leads

When we submit to the leading and guidance of the Holy Spirit, He helps us become more holy—more like Jesus. It is a lifelong journey of putting our flesh to death, or as Paul puts it in Galatians 5, of walking by the Spirit and not gratifying the desires of the flesh. We cannot live submitted to the Spirit and at the same time gratify the flesh because these two "are opposed to each other" (Gal. 5:17). The works of the flesh are things like strife, fits of anger, dissensions, and idolatry. The works of the Spirit are things like love, self-control, joy, and faithfulness. Obviously, these are very different from each other. In making this distinction, Paul goes so far as to say that those who belong to Christ "have crucified the flesh with its passions and desires" (5:24).

The phrase *crucifying the flesh* is not exactly a friendly, appealing group of words. I think this is because God wants us to be clear on what we are getting into. He wants us to know that His gift of the Holy Spirit is really not for our own pleasure or purposes. The Spirit is meant to lead us toward holiness. The Spirit is here with us to accomplish God's purposes, not ours.

When you decide to put to death—to crucify—your flesh, you are by default choosing the way of the Spirit. You are leaving one path and joining another. The new path of walking with the Spirit will undoubtedly have its share of twists and turns. At forks in the trail, you will, at times, choose to follow the desires of your flesh, even though you left that path long ago.

The way of the Spirit is not a gentle downhill grade. Often, walking with the Spirit is an uphill trudge through all sorts of distractions and difficulties. But while the path is winding and difficult, you are constantly moving in a particular direction, and that direction is set by the leading of the Spirit. At some point along the way, you agreed with God that you were not meant to be ruled by your fleshly desires and passions (like anger, self-indulgence, immorality, etc.), and you removed the central role that these things once had in your life.

Perhaps you have not yet made this decision. Understand that it is a decision everyone must make. It cannot be done mindlessly, not when we are talking about something as intense as crucifying. Each of us has to decide whether we are going to crucify the flesh, whether we will truly walk with the Spirit. It is a choice. And it is crucial.

———————

In addition to becoming like Christ in His holiness, being led by the Spirit will result in becoming like Christ in His love. After Paul addresses the manifestations or gifts that the Spirit gives, he writes, "I will show you a still more excellent way" (1 Cor. 12:31). It's as if he is saying, "Sure, these gifts from the Spirit are important. But let me tell you what is really important. Let me tell you about what will change the world." And in chapter 13 of that letter, he writes his famous "love chapter." In it he reminds us that without love, nothing else matters.

> If I speak in the tongues of men and of angels, but have not love, I am a noisy gong or a clanging cymbal. And if I have prophetic powers, and understand all mysteries and all knowledge, and if I have all faith, so as to remove mountains, but have not love, I am nothing. If I give away all I have, and if I deliver up my body to be burned, but have not love, I gain nothing. (13:1–3)

This passage is so powerful because Paul redirects the focus from supernatural gifts to love. He specifically says that without love, speaking "in the tongues of men and of angels" and "prophetic powers" and understanding "all mysteries and all knowledge" mean nothing.

The Holy Spirit is the one who fills believers with God's love and the one who enables us to love one another. Paul describes this beautifully in his prayer to the Ephesians:

> I pray that out of his glorious riches he may strengthen you with power *through his Spirit* in your inner being, so that Christ may dwell in your hearts through faith. And I pray that you, being *rooted and established in love*, may have power, together with all the saints, to grasp how wide and long and high and deep is the love of Christ, and to know this love that surpasses knowledge—that you may be filled to the measure of all the fullness of God. (3:16–19 NIV)

May we know this love that surpasses knowledge—the mystery of this great love—by the strengthening power of the Spirit.

Let us not become distracted from what is most important. Jesus told His disciples, "Behold, I have given you authority to tread on serpents and scorpions, and over all the power of the enemy, and nothing shall hurt you. Nevertheless, do not rejoice in this, that the spirits are subject to you, but rejoice that your names are written in heaven" (Luke 10:19–20). Our true rejoicing comes because of the grace that's been given to us.

And like our Savior, who poured out His life and blood so we have reason to rejoice, we were made to lay down our lives and give until it hurts. We are most alive when we are loving and actively giving of ourselves because we were made to do these things. It is when we live like this that the Spirit of God moves and acts in and through us in ways that on our own we are not capable of. This is our purpose for living. This is our hope. "And hope does not put us to shame, because God's love has been poured out into our hearts through the Holy Spirit who has been given to us" (Rom. 5:5).

Esther Ahn Kim

Esther Ahn Kim's biography is among the most powerful testimonies I have ever read. It was during WWII, and the Japanese occupation of Korea, that Esther's journey of faith really began. She refused to bow down at the shrines set up in every corner of her country and was eventually imprisoned for six years, from 1939 until 1945.

Knowing she was destined for prison for refusing to bow to idols, Esther spent time training herself both physically and spiritually. Each day she would find and eat food that was decaying, knowing that was what she would be served in prison. The discipline she demonstrated is humbling; how many of us would *choose* to eat rotten foods?

While preparing for prison, she memorized more than one hundred chapters of the Bible and many hymns because she knew she would not be allowed to keep her Bible. She spent countless hours seeking God through fasting and prayer. These times when she read the Scriptures led to greater clarity, and she was able to surrender her fear of being tortured.

Reading her story left me wanting more. More intimacy with Christ. More love for people. More of God in my life. And to be honest, more discipline. She was a well-disciplined believer, but there was nothing self-righteous about her. Her obedience to Christ only increased her ability to hear the voice of the Spirit, and consequently filled her with overwhelming love for the people she came in contact with.

When she eventually was taken to prison, God used her in countless way. One night a young Chinese woman convicted of killing her husband was brought in. She moaned incessantly and beat on the doors until the guards tied her hands behind her back. It was this woman that God called Esther to love and reach out to. Esther held the woman's feet at night to warm them, even though the woman was covered in her own excrement. Though food rations were small, Esther gave up her portions for three days to this woman.

Over time, the Chinese woman began to respond, carrying on conversation and eventually accepting the good news of the gospel. The woman was later executed for her crime, but she went to her death alive in Christ.

This is one of many people God used Esther to minister to. Murderers and swindlers who were utter outcasts were changed before all who watched as the love of Christ, through Esther, healed their hearts and gave them hope. Even the jailers and government officials noticed how Esther shone in that dark place. She could have just endured her suffering like a good Christian, and we would have applauded her for it. But she was not content to merely endure. She was ready every day and every moment, asking God, "Who do You want me to love for You today?"[3]

CHAPTER 5

A Real Relationship

When we are at our wits' end for an
answer, then the Holy Spirit can give us
an answer. But how can He give us an
answer when we are still well supplied
with all sorts of answers of our own?

-Karl Barth-

There's nothing worse than insecurity. So many people live in fear because they are uncertain about what comes next and their standing before God, if they even believe in God. On the flip side, there's nothing better than being absolutely sure that the most powerful Being in the universe adores you as His own child. This is precisely the confidence the Holy Spirit offers us.

Serving God and living faithfully can become a constant guilt trip of "trying harder" and "doing better next time." Maybe you can relate. I have spent much of my Christian life battling insecurity, never quite feeling sure of my salvation, living out of fear and a desperate determination to earn acceptance.

I was raised in a home where performance was everything. Unconditional love may have existed, but I never saw it. Failure was met with severe consequences. Dad was my authority; that was all there was to it. I'm not one to blame my lack of faith on circumstances, but our upbringings definitely create challenges for us. Some of you have wounds so deep that you wonder if you'll ever be able to trust. Perhaps you've subconsciously taken the failures from sinful human relationships and imposed those shortcomings onto a perfect God. Now uncertainty creeps into even your relationship with God.

It is the Holy Spirit who keeps us from this path and gives us confidence so we can enjoy intimacy with our Creator. Though I do not believe God gives us His Spirit solely for our personal benefit, it is undeniable that one of the greatest aspects of being in relationship with the Holy Spirit is the intimacy, security, and encouragement He brings us. It is then we can serve God as a beloved child rather than a stressed-out, guilt-ridden slave.

A study through Galatians helped me discover and destroy the strongholds of earning and insecurity. And it was while preaching the book of Galatians that I learned to enjoy being "known" by God.

> But now that you have come to know God, or rather
> to be known by God, how can you turn back again
> to the weak and worthless elementary principles of
> the world, whose slaves you want to be once more?
> (Gal. 4:9)

Have you ever thought about what it means to be "known"? Though I'd been telling people for years that I "knew" God, only recently have I explored the concept of being "known" by Him. It's breathtaking to picture almighty God saying, "I know Francis Chan. He's my son. I love him!" Are you confident this is what God would say if I asked Him about you? Do you know God or just know about Him? Are you acquaintances or intimate friends?

In Galatians 4, Paul explains the difference between a slave and a child. His desire was to ensure that the Galatians were enjoying the rightful privileges Christ earned for them on the cross. Many of us would say that we are children of God, but are these empty words for you? Can you say with confidence—from the depth of your being—that you know God and are known by Him?

Paul tells the Galatians that the Holy Spirit is the one who assures our hearts that we are His children: "Because you are his sons, God sent the Spirit of his Son into our hearts, the Spirit who calls out, 'Abba, Father.' So you are no longer slaves, but God's children; and since you are his children, he has made you also heirs." (4:6–7 TNIV).

These verses speak an amazing, beautiful truth! I can't fully explain it, but I've often experienced it in intimate moments with God. This is one of the precious gifts the Holy Spirit gives us. He assures us that we are in right standing with and loved by God. He guarantees believers of the gift of new life in Christ. He assures us that we have nothing to fear because we are His children and He is powerful. He tells us that we are accepted, fully and unconditionally. And He reminds us of the victory that is coming when God's kingdom is fully realized.

Paul emphasized these critical truths in his letter to the Romans:

> For you did not receive the spirit of slavery to fall back into fear, but you have received the Spirit of adoption as sons, by whom we cry, "Abba! Father!" The Spirit himself bears witness with our spirit that we are children of God, and if children, then heirs—heirs of God and fellow heirs with Christ, provided we suffer with him in order that we may also be glorified with him. (Rom. 8:15–17)

I don't know where you are as you read this. Perhaps you're tracking 100 percent and just want to voice your affirmation. If that's you, then I say, "Amen!" Maybe you are reading this and are thinking, *Well, I just don't experience that kind of intimacy with God … the Spirit in me never cries "Abba! Father!"* If this is you, I don't have a four-step guide to connecting with the Holy Spirit. I would, however, like to suggest two potential obstacles for you to consider: comfort and volume.

Comfort (Maybe Your Life Is Too Safe)

From my own experience, I have felt closest to God when nearness to Him was a necessity. The Bible says that the Spirit comes through in situations where we would normally be afraid (Luke 12:11–12). We experience the Holy Spirit guiding us in desperate situations, such as being placed on trial for the gospel (in some countries), when we are asked why we believe in a God that allows _____ (fill in the world's most recent tragic horror) to happen, or when we receive a totally unexpected phone call that a close family member has died.

Jesus refers to the Holy Spirit as the "Helper" or "Comforter." Let me ask you a simple question: Why would we need to experience the Comforter if our lives are already comfortable? It is those who put their lives at risk and suffer for the gospel (Phil. 1:29) who will most often experience His being "with you always, even to the end of the age" (Matt. 28:20 NASB). Though this verse is true for all believers (of course God is always with us), if we are never alone or feeling like we need Him, how much do we care or need to know that God is with us?

I recently had dinner in Seoul, Korea, with an amazing man. He was one of the twenty-three missionaries who were held hostage by the Taliban in Afghanistan in July 2007. For those who don't recall the story, the Taliban executed two of the missionaries before a deal was reached with the government of South Korea and the missionaries were released.

This man told me about the horrors of being locked up in a cell, knowing that martyrdom was a strong possibility. He also shared about the amazing time they had on the last day they were all imprisoned together (their captors later divided them into groups of three and took them to remote areas). Each of the twenty-three missionaries surrendered their lives to God that night and told Him they were willing to die for His glory. There was even an argument over who would *get* to die first. One of them had a small Bible that the missionaries secretly ripped into twenty-three pieces so each could glance at Scripture when no one was watching. The Word of God and the Spirit of God got them through the forty days of imprisonment.

One of the most fascinating things this man told me was about what has happened since. Now that they have been back in Seoul for a while, several team members have asked him, "Don't you wish we were still there?" He tells me that several of them experienced a deep kind of intimacy with God in the prison cell that they haven't been able to recapture in their comfort.

This is the precious gift of intimacy the Holy Spirit offers us. It is a security that is priceless and worth any loss of safety and comfort, even imprisonment by the Taliban.

Volume (Maybe Your Life Is Too Loud)

Multitasking has become the norm. When was the last time you had an uninterrupted conversation with anyone? No phones, text messages, or to-do lists running through your mind. It's so rare nowadays to be able to look someone in the eye without interruption or distraction. A while back, I found myself talking on the phone, emailing on my laptop, and playing Wii with my daughter all at once. In my quest to accomplish much, I've lost the art of focusing on one thing or one person. This in turn has affected my prayer life, as I'm sure it has affected yours. I find it harder to simply be with God, to focus only on Him while spending intentional time with Him.

While Jesus didn't have to deal with emails, voice mails, or texts, He certainly understood what it meant to have multitudes of people pursuing Him at once. At any given moment of the day, people were looking for Jesus. Because of the priority of His relationship with His Father, He found ways to escape. He took the time to focus and be quiet (Mark 1:35). He was willing to remove Himself from people's reach in order to pray and commune with God the Father. Our lack of intimacy often is due to our refusal to unplug and shut off communication from all others so we can be alone with Him.

In the craziness of our world, it takes tremendous effort to find a quiet place. It takes time to quiet your mind and your heart before the Lord. It means turning off the music, the television, or your cell phone. It might mean going outside to your favorite spot. For some, this is curling up inside in the only place where you find privacy. For others it might mean heading to whatever wilderness is nearest to you or booking a few days at a local retreat center.

I don't know exactly what it will look like for you to be still before the Lord. But I do know that no matter what your personality, it is a spiritual discipline to be still, to listen, and to cut out the distraction and din of our world. And as we practice this stillness, this waiting, this being, it is then that we can experience deep intimacy and relationship with the Holy Spirit.

For some of you, reading this book could be a form of noise that keeps you from Him. Maybe you already hear lots of sermons and read plenty of books. What you need is direct communion with Him—to hear directly from Him and to speak directly to Him. Rather than reading my words, listen to His.

Right now I want you to take a break and open your Bible to the book of John. Read chapters 14 through 16 and give yourself some space to soak in the words you read. Notice particularly how Christ desires that His disciples have peace and how He comforts His disciples with the truth that they are not left alone. Part of His answer to how we are to have peace and be comforted is through the provision of the Holy Spirit, the other Counselor, who He promised would come once He left.

⎯⎯⎯⎯⎯⎯

It makes sense that Jesus would say it's to our advantage to have this "other counselor." After all, Jesus merely walked beside the disciples; the Spirit would actually enter their human bodies (John 14:17). You've probably heard this truth a hundred times, but have you marveled at it? Would you be willing to take thirty seconds right now just to dwell on the fact that God is *in* you?

Astonished? This is not a distant, loose connection. This is the Spirit of God choosing you and me to be His dwelling place. That means that as I write, the Spirit of the living God is inside me. I might wake up on a particular day feeling physically tired or stressed or impatient, and humanly speaking, those things would probably define my day. But the reality is that I am indwelt by the Holy Spirit. And because of this reality, stress and tiredness and impatience don't have to define my day.

If you have received by faith the promise of the Holy Spirit, you are also His temple. As you drive your children to school. As you go to work every day. As you embark on a new, unknown season. As you go to school. As you face tragedy and pain. As you buy groceries. As you give of yourself in relationships. As you walk the dog. As you make decisions. As you live your life, the Holy Spirit is dwelling in you.

Please don't let this reality slip past you like an interesting piece of trivia that might catch your attention for a minute but that you'll never take the time to really investigate. You are a temple of the Holy Spirit. You are not just a person living your life by human power. The Spirit of God is in you; that is why Jesus said it was better for Him to go and the Spirit to come. Don't walk away from this. Delve into it and let it impact you deeply, first internally and then outwardly.

Those chapters in John, where we read of Christ's compassion for and care of His disciples, are but one small example of the meaningful relationship and deep love that motivate God's interaction with us. In Galatians 3, we read that "Christ redeemed us from the curse of the law by becoming a curse for us … so that we might receive the promised Spirit through faith" (vv. 13–14). Wow. I am sure I have read that often enough, but until I started paying attention to the Holy Spirit, I am not sure that it really struck me. Christ redeemed us from the curse we were under *so that* we could receive the promise of the Holy Spirit. The "promised Spirit" is not a small promise. Jesus suffered a grueling death *so that* I could have the amazing gift of the Holy Spirit. How dare I take this for granted?

Because of Jesus, I have received the promise. And this Spirit is not a remote force. He takes up residence in our lives, in our very bodies, and by doing so brings with Him a deep level of security. Again and again in the Scriptures we read about being God's children, being led by His Spirit, and how we have received the Spirit of adoption.

Kristen has been a friend of the family for the past ten years. I'll never forget being with her at her mother's memorial service. As I watched her grieve, there was no doubt that she was loved by this woman who had adopted her from Korea. She was Kristen's mother, not just some lady who looked after her and paid for her food. It's been years since her death, yet Kristen still has a hard time talking about her without getting emotional. She misses Mom. This is the type of adoption God speaks of in Scripture. It's not about having an impersonal guardian who looks over you. It's about having a parent. The best parent there ever was or will be.

We have been chosen, grafted, adopted into the family of God. And now that we are a part of the family, the Spirit causes us to call out, "Abba! Father!" Remember that Abba is the most intimate form for referring to a father. It is like saying "Daddy"; it connotes a deep level of familiarity and intimacy. As God's Spirit speaks to our hearts, we can call out to God as our Abba. We will begin to experience this intimate relationship more deeply than we ever thought possible, so much so that we will begin to wonder, *Does everyone feel this loved by God?*

Don't let your personal baggage keep you from enjoying this intimacy that both your spirit and God's long for. I had issues that kept me from crying out to Abba. I often wished my testimony was like those of the drug addicts or criminals who came to know the Lord and then completely changed their lifestyles. Unlike them, I was raised in a Christian home and came to know Jesus personally in high school. After several years of walking with Him, I began to turn. I went through my sinful phase after knowing better and after having received the Holy Spirit. I quenched the conviction the Holy Spirit put in my heart over and over again.

I can totally relate to the prodigal son after he squandered his wealth (Luke 15:11–32). I resonate with the feelings he had when he was eating with the pigs, thinking he could go back to the father as a slave. Sometimes I waited a few days or even weeks before talking to Him because I wanted to have a period of proving myself. In doing this, I acted like a slave and obeyed as well as I could. I figured I could still serve Him even though I felt uncomfortable having a real conversation with Him.

Have you ever felt this way? Do you ever want to distance yourself from Him because you feel so much shame over your sin?

This was a regular pattern for me. I wanted to prove that I was sorry for what I did by being faithful for a period of time. I wanted to develop a good track record before pursuing my relationship with Him again. I wanted God to see that I could be a good servant. *Then* I felt good enough to talk with God again. But God didn't want a good slave who tried really hard. He wanted me to see that He was a good Father. He wants intimacy.

It takes faith to believe God is truly like the prodigal son's father, who from afar "saw him and felt compassion, and ran and embraced him and kissed him" (Luke 15:20). Lest there be any doubt, the father made it absolutely clear that his son was to be forgiven, with no questions asked. He invited his son back into his life without bitterness or requiring penance and guilt.

In the same way, the Spirit speaks truth to our hearts, such as "there is now no condemnation for those who are in Christ Jesus" (Rom. 8:1 NIV) and "[nothing] will be able to separate us from the love of God that is in Christ Jesus" (Rom. 8:39 NIV) and "He is faithful and righteous to forgive us our sins" (1 John 1:9 NASB). These are verses we could probably spout off, but often we need reminding of the power and veracity of them. And one of the Holy Spirit's roles is to do this reminding.

God said to Israel, "You will seek me and find me, when you seek me with all your heart. I will be found by you, declares the LORD" (Jer. 29:13–14). When is the last time you sought after God with *all* your heart? We are not Israel, but God still desires to be sought and found by His people. Ask the Holy Spirit to enable you to set *everything* else aside right now so that you can seek Him wholeheartedly. Tell God that you want intimacy with Him, no matter what, even if it necessitates suffering on your part. When this relationship with Him is as it should be, there is nothing more satisfying or meaningful.

Thomas and Jen Yun

Have you ever met people who are so joyful and kind you assume they are fake? After all, no one could genuinely be *that* cheerful, certainly not all the time. Thomas and Jen would be the first to admit their imperfections. But I secretly wish I could see those come out more so I would feel less guilty about myself.

Jen works in our church office, and she's one of the people I think of when I hear the term *Spirit-filled*. She doesn't have a list of accomplishments to amaze you. It is more about who she is than what she's done. I think you know the type—the person who convicts you just by how she lives her life and interacts with people.

I first met Thomas because he was a chef and co-owner of an extremely nice and expensive steak house in town. He sent a gift certificate to my wife and me so we could enjoy a meal that most pastors can't afford. While we were there, Thomas shared with me how great the restaurant was doing. It had far exceeded expectations.

In another three years he would receive back not only his initial investment but a huge bonus on top of that. The only problem was that God was calling him away from the restaurant then, not in three years.

Thomas surprised his partners by giving up the money in order to pursue the ministry God was calling him to. Thomas left the fancy restaurant and took a position at the local rescue mission. He now cooks for the homeless, recovering addicts, and others who are seeking to rebuild their lives. He uses his training in the culinary arts to teach the homeless how to cook. He then helps them find jobs as cooks at local restaurants.

Thomas and Jen are a young couple in our church body; they are a Spirit-filled and Spirit-led couple. They believe God will soon call them overseas, but until that day comes, they seek daily to follow as the Spirit leads. And they are doing it.

CHAPTER 6

Forget About His Will for Your Life!

And to expose our hearts to truth and consistently
refuse or neglect to obey the impulses it arouses
is to stymie the motions of life within us and, if
persisted in, to grieve the Holy Spirit into silence.

-A.W. Tozer-

How many times have you heard someone say, "I just wish I knew God's will for my life"? I know I've longed for this before. But now I see it as a misguided way of thinking and talking.

There are very few people in the Scriptures who received their life plan from God in advance (or even their five-year plan, for that matter!). Consider Abraham, who was told to pack up his family and all his possessions and start walking. He didn't know where he was going. He didn't know if he would ever be back. He didn't know any of the details we consider vital (e.g., his destination, how long the venture would take, what the costs/rewards would be, whether he'd receive a 401(k) or health insurance). God said to go and he went, and that's pretty much all he knew.

I think a lot of us need to forget about *God's will for my life*. God cares more about our response to His Spirit's leading today, in this moment, than about what we intend to do next year. In fact, the decisions we make next year will be profoundly affected by the degree to which we submit to the Spirit right now, in today's decisions.

It is easy to use the phrase "God's will for my life" as an excuse for inaction or even disobedience. It's much less demanding to think about God's will for your future than it is to ask Him what He wants you to do in the next ten minutes. It's safer to commit to following Him *someday* instead of *this day*.

To be honest, I believe part of the desire to "know God's will for my life" is birthed in fear and results in paralysis. We are scared to make mistakes, so we fret over figuring out God's will. We wonder what living according to His will would actually look and feel like, and we are scared to find out. We forget that we were never promised a twenty-year plan of action; instead, God promises multiple times in Scripture never to leave or forsake us.

God wants us to listen to His Spirit on a daily basis, and even throughout the day, as difficult and stretching moments arise, and in the midst of the mundane. My hope is that instead of searching for

"God's will for my life," each of us would learn to seek hard after "the Spirit's leading in my life today." May we learn to pray for an open and willing heart, to surrender to the Spirit's leading with that friend, child, spouse, circumstance, or decision in our lives right now.

To say that we are not called to figure out "God's will for my life" does not mean God doesn't have purposes and plans for each of our lives or that He doesn't care what we do with our lives. He does. In both the Old and New Testaments He tells us that this is true. The key is that He never promises to reveal these purposes all at once, in advance.

We do know that we are called to keep in step with the Holy Spirit. In Paul's letter to the Galatians we read, "But I say, walk by the Spirit, and you will not gratify the desires of the flesh.... If we live by the Spirit, let us also walk by the Spirit" (5:16, 25).

The phrases *keeping in step with the Spirit* and *walking with the Spirit* are mostly likely familiar, but do they affect your life in a practical and meaningful way? Like I said earlier, I think dwelling on God's plan for the future often excuses us from faithful and sacrificial living now. It tends to create a safe zone of sorts, where we can sit around and have "spiritual" conversations about what God "might" have planned for our lives. Thinking, questioning, and talking can take the place of letting the Spirit affect our immediate actions in radical ways. God wants to see His children stake everything on His power and presence in their lives.

Nowhere in Scripture do I see a "balanced life with a little bit of God added in" as an ideal for us to emulate. Yet when I look at our churches, this is exactly what I see: a lot of people who have added Jesus to their lives. People who have, in a sense, asked Him to join them on *their* life journey, to follow *them* wherever *they* feel they should go, rather than following Him as we are commanded. The God of the universe is not something we can just add to our lives and keep on as we did before. The Spirit who raised Christ from the dead is not someone we can just call on when we want a little extra power in our lives. Jesus Christ did not die in order to follow *us*. He died and rose again so that we could forget everything else and follow Him to the cross, to true Life.

When people give their lives to God in exchange for a ticket out of hell, there is often no turning or change of direction, which is the definition of repentance. If all you want is a little Jesus to "spiritualize" your life, a little extra God to keep you out of hell, you are missing out on the fullness of life you were created for.

Not only this, you don't need the Holy Spirit. You don't need the Holy Spirit if you are merely seeking to live a semi-moral life and attend church regularly. You can find people of all sorts in many religions doing that quite nicely without Him. You only need the Holy Spirit's guidance and help if you truly want to follow the Way of Jesus Christ. You only need Him if you desire to "obey everything" He commanded and to teach others to do the same (Matt. 28:18–20 NIV). You only need the Holy Spirit if you have genuinely repented and believe. And you only need the Holy Spirit if you understand that you are called to share in Christ's suffering and death, as well as

His resurrection (Rom. 8:17; 2 Cor. 4:16–18; Phil. 3:10–11). Paul demonstrated this when he wrote,

> But we have this treasure in jars of clay to show that this all-surpassing power is from God and not from us. We are hard pressed on every side, but not crushed; perplexed, but not in despair; persecuted, but not abandoned; struck down, but not destroyed. We always carry around in our body the death of Jesus, so that the life of Jesus may also be revealed in our body. For we who are alive are always being given over to death for Jesus' sake, so that his life may also be revealed in our mortal body. (2 Cor. 4:7–11 NIV)

If you truly believe and have turned from the way you were headed and joined a different Way of living, then you desperately need the Holy Spirit. You know you cannot live this Way without the Spirit in you.

I think repentance is one of those words we hear a lot but maybe don't incorporate into our lives very often. When I use the word *repent,* I think about the time I was in a dating relationship, until one day a girl named Lisa came to my church as a guest soloist and caught my attention. After getting to know her, I knew she was the one I wanted to be with. I didn't consider it an option to ask Lisa if she wanted to date me *also*. I knew I had to break off the other relationship if I wanted to begin one with Lisa.

In a sense, this is what repentance is like when we meet Jesus: We totally change direction.

Some people encounter Jesus and say, "Sweet! Jesus, do You want to join the party of my life with this sin, that addiction, this destructive relationship, and we'll all just coexist together?" But repentance means saying, "Sweet Jesus, You are the best thing that has ever happened to me! I want to turn from all the sin and selfishness that rules me. I want to let it go and walk with You. Only You. You are my life now. Help me to walk away from the enslaving, worthless things in life."

Do you see the difference between these two examples? Which do you think more accurately portrays your own life? Is there anything you need to go and make right with your Savior, the One who was killed for your sake? If so, don't hesitate to shut this book and spend the necessary time. Nothing else matters more than this relationship.

So if a little bit of spirituality added in to our lives is not what God has in mind, what does He want for His children? How does He desire that we live? The fact is we were called by Jesus to give up everything. His call is to come and take up the cross (Luke 9:23).

"Taking up my cross" has become a euphemism for getting through life's typical burdens with a semi-good attitude. Yet life's typical burdens—busy schedules, bills, illness, hard decisions, paying for college tuition, losing jobs, houses not selling, and the family dog dying—are felt by everyone, whether or not they follow the Way of Jesus.

When Jesus calls us to take up our cross, He is doing much more than calling us to endure the daily, circumstantial troubles of life. The people in Jesus' day were very familiar with the cross. Having witnessed crucifixion, they understood the commitment and sacrifice of taking up a cross.

It is a call to radical faith.

Jesus is calling us to be willing to suffer anything and forsake everything for the sake of the gospel. His call is to love those who have cheated us in business; those who have spread nasty rumors about us; those who would kill us if they could; those who disagree with us politically, practically, and fundamentally. His call is to consider everything a loss for His sake. His call is for total surrender. He calls us to give up all that we have, to give even to the point of offering up our lives as a living sacrifice. His call means realizing that His power is made perfect in our weakness, that when we are weak we are also strong (2 Cor. 12:9–10).

Do you remember the story where Jesus saw people putting gifts into the offering box? At first some rich people gave, and it sounds like their contributions must have been monetarily large. Then Jesus pointed out a widow (the text even says a "poor widow") who put in two small copper coins. Notice Christ's words in response to what he witnessed: "Truly, I tell you, this poor widow has put in more than all of them. For they all contributed out of their abundance, but she out of her poverty put in all she had to live on" (Luke 21:3–4). Jesus commends this woman, whom the world—those people with power and money—overlooked and perhaps even derided. Jesus praises her for her revolutionary faith, for holding nothing back. She literally gave everything she had, even though she was a "poor widow" with no other means of income or support. And Jesus holds her up as an example.

What if you could hear the voice of the Holy Spirit and He asked you to literally give *everything* you owned? What if He asked you to sell *all* your possessions and give the money to the poor? Could you do it? Before you start explaining why He would never ask that of you, take a moment and answer the question honestly. It's not out of His character to ask for everything.

I don't know about you, but that challenges me like crazy. I say I want to give it all to God, to truly submit myself to the leading of the Holy Spirit. But I won't lie; sometimes the reality of what that means leaves me wanting to hold back a little. There are things on this earth that I *really* enjoy, like surfing, golfing, eating out, and laughing with friends. I know what you're thinking: that those things are not sinful. And you are right. But that doesn't mean the Spirit will not lead me to forgo those things occasionally or maybe even permanently for His purposes and the glory of the Father.

I struggle to always and actually keep in step with the Spirit moment by moment. To submit and give up everything truly is radical and terrifying. However, when I think deeply about it, walking in my own wisdom, contrary to the Spirit's leading, is even more frightful. Though I struggle, I know that ultimately I want nothing more than to live in total surrender and abandonment to the Spirit every moment I have left on this earth.

The Spirit may lead me into total sacrifice financially, or He may lead me toward humiliation in the opinions of people around me.

The Spirit may ask me to move to a different city, a different state, or a different country. The Spirit may ask me to stay where I am and spend my time in very different ways than I do now. He could lead me toward actions like in 2 Samuel 6, where David danced (it says in "a linen ephod," the equivalent of priestly underwear) before the Lord "with all his might" (v. 14). Others were shamed by his undignified display of worship to God, yet David said that he didn't care and that he would become even more undignified for the sake of the Lord. All he cared about was worshipping his God.

When I read this story, part of me says, "Yes, I want to live like David. I want to forget about what others think and worship my King with all of me." The other part of me says, "Okay, but practically, what does that look like?" How do I walk in such intimacy with the Spirit that my genuine response when He moves is to dance with abandon, heedless of those around me who might consider it inappropriate? And do I really need not to care about what others think of me?

The crux of it, I believe, is realizing that being filled with the Spirit is not a one-time act. As we read in Galatians about the Spirit and the flesh, walking with the Spirit implies an ongoing relationship. Being filled with the Spirit is not limited to the day we first meet Christ. Instead, throughout Scripture we read of a relationship that calls us into an active pursuit of the Spirit.

Christians can't ever lose the Spirit, but His filling is something we should constantly pursue. This business of sanctification is a lifelong process we are engaged in. Second Corinthians 3:18 says, "We all, who with unveiled faces contemplate the Lord's glory, are being transformed into his image with ever-increasing glory, which comes from the Lord, who is the Spirit" (TNIV). (See also 2 Thess. 2:13 and Rom. 15:16.)

Imagine I buy a treadmill to lose some weight. Three months later I take it back to the store and complain to the clerk that it didn't work—I didn't lose a pound. He asks me, "What was the problem? Did it not work properly?" I respond, "I don't know if it works. I never ran on it. I just know I didn't lose any weight, so I am done with it!"

This may seem like a silly example, but change the details and suddenly it sounds pretty familiar:

"I have prayed for the Holy Spirit to free me from my lust, and I am still addicted to pornography." Or, "I have prayed for years to be able to forgive my dad, but I am still racked with anger and bitterness thirty years down the road." "I have prayed for years to be free of my gluttony, but despite prayer, spiritually based support groups, and dieting, I am still a compulsive, unhealthy eater." Fill in whatever sin plagues you and suddenly the treadmill illustration doesn't seem so silly. In fact, it seems like those prayers for freedom from that ongoing sin didn't really "work" in much the same way the treadmill didn't help me lose any weight.

Receiving freedom and healing in answer to prayer is generally not something that is done to you, a situation in which you are just a passive participant. Occasionally God works this way and simply heals or frees a person outright. He is certainly capable of this. But in my experience, He typically asks us to play an active role in the journey toward wholeness. He doesn't need our help but invites us to participate. Often this journey to freedom takes time, sometimes a very long time. And it takes perseverance. It takes participation on our part. We have to get on the treadmill and run—merely looking at the workout machine doesn't do a whole lot. (See also Rom. 12:11 and 1 Thess. 5:19.)

Have you been stuck in a cycle of sin for a long time? Have you given up on the Holy Spirit and resigned yourself to thinking that He doesn't "work" or doesn't have the power to bring freedom, at least not in your life? If this is you, then maybe you have not internalized the reality that walking in the Spirit requires action on your part.

Because the fact is that if you were in step with the Holy Spirit, listening to and obeying Him, you wouldn't sin (Gal. 5:16). In any given moment, it is impossible to live in the power of the Spirit and sin at the same time. Sin is wholly opposed to everything that is of the Spirit. They really are mutually exclusive and totally contrary to each other.

This does not mean that if you sin, you don't have the Holy Spirit or aren't a follower of Christ. It does mean that when you are sinning, you are not simultaneously submitted to the authority and presence of the Holy Spirit in your life. He is still present, but you are most likely suppressing or ignoring His counsel.

The hopeful part in all this is that even when we do ignore the Spirit and sin, the Holy Spirit convicts us of that sin. Though at times we sin, we are not ruled and enslaved by sin as we once were. We have cut off the headship of sin in our lives. When we are attuned to the Spirit, we are reminded of this freeing reality.

It's obvious when someone is not walking in the Spirit (at least not consistently). What you see and experience from such a person is usually along the lines of rage, selfishness, dissension, bitterness, and envy. However, when a person is habitually and actively submitted to the Spirit, what comes out of his or her life is the fruit of the Spirit. The Holy Spirit will not—*cannot*—lead you into sin. If the Holy Spirit is in you, as a believer, then when you sin you are not listening to the Spirit's leading.

—————

Haven't you met those rare people who you can tell are daily keeping in step with the Spirit? Somehow they exude graciousness and peacefulness to a degree that is not humanly possible. Don't you want that in your own life? I mean, who really wants to be a stressed-out, angry, selfish person? It's not much fun, for you or anyone who happens to come in contact with you.

Several people in my own life come to mind when I think about people who walk with the Spirit daily. It would be easy to start comparing ourselves to others in this area. I can already hear the thought progression: *Well, I am obviously more Spirit-led than* that *person....*

Instead of wasting time deliberating over whether others are walking with the Spirit (which is definitely *not* our job), I challenge you to examine yourself. Look at the "fruit" of your own life and let it be a gauge for you of your own connectedness with the Spirit. Do you listen to the Holy Spirit as you stand in line at the post office? Perhaps He is asking you to begin a conversation with the elderly lady in front of you. Do you allow the Holy Spirit to lead when you are making your budget? Perhaps He will direct you to allocate the monies differently than you otherwise would. Do you submit to the Holy Spirit as you spend time with your family? Often it is family members who are most difficult to love, and we need the Spirit's help to love them well. These are just a few of the many, many areas of our lives that we can submit to the Spirit's leading. Take some time to think about areas in your own life where you tend just to do your own thing, heedless of the Spirit's will and call.

Living by the Spirit implies a habitual, continual, and active interaction with the Holy Spirit. While this sounds exhausting, it really isn't because all of this living and action is done in the power of the Spirit. It is not by your own strength.

This, however, brings up a whole other confusing issue: Is it God's work or my work? God's responsibility or mine? Paul addresses this when he writes to the Galatians. He calls them out, asking whom they had been bewitched by (quite an accusation!). He asks, "Having begun by the Spirit, are you now being perfected by the flesh?" (3:3).

I think each of us has a strong tendency to attempt to wrestle control from the Spirit and "do" this life on our own. Each of us tends to switch from living the gospel of grace to trusting in a system of works. That's why Paul brings up this issue with the churches in Galatia. He knows it's hard to truly depend on sustenance and guidance from the Spirit rather than merely on our own wisdom and effort.

Remember the treadmill illustration? Perhaps you wonder how the concept of our actions fits in with the gospel of grace, which cannot be merited or earned. Suppose I bake a loaf of bread and you asked me, "Which ingredient is more important, the yeast or the flour?" I would look at my still-warm loaf of bread and reply that both are fundamentally necessary to the making of bread; you simply would not have bread without both yeast and flour.

This illustration bears a similarity to our spiritual lives. If we never responded to God, if we never acted based on what He has done for us, there wouldn't be much of a relationship there. God is still real and moving, but at some point we have to respond and act because of what He's done. Like yeast and flour are both necessary to bread, both God's action and our response-action are necessary in this relationship with God.

In the book of Philippians, Paul writes, "Therefore, my beloved, as you have always obeyed, so now, not only as in my presence but much more in my absence, work out your own salvation with fear and trembling, for it is God who works in you, both to will and to work for his good pleasure" (2:12–13). I love the apparent contradiction in this passage. Paul says in one breath, "Work out your own salvation," and in the next, "It is God who works in you." The both-ness here doesn't allow us to escape with a simple conclusion. Yes, it is God who works in you. And, yes, there is work for you to do. Yes, the Spirit empowers you to do the work. And, yes, you do the work.

Like many things in life, there really isn't a sew-it-all-up solution. And I love that. God is big and mysterious enough that we cannot simply put a label on this process and move on. It requires continual engagement and wrestling and discovering how to live a Spirit-filled life today. Not ten years from now. Not tomorrow. But right now, in the particular time and place He has put us. As we "work out our salvation" and as "God works in us." Let us keep in step.

Dave Phillips

Years ago, Dave Phillips and his wife, Lynn, had a talk about the callings they felt God was stirring in them. As they discussed what they were most passionate about, they agreed that bringing relief to suffering children and reaching the next generation with the gospel were at the top of the list. The thought of starting a relief agency was considered, but Dave's response was, "But that would mean I have to talk in front of people." By nature, Dave is a very quiet, behind-the-scenes man.

But after much prayer, Dave set aside his fears, and he and Lynn started Children's Hunger Fund out of their garage. Six weeks after CHF was launched, in January of 1992, he received a phone call from the director of a cancer treatment center in Honduras asking if there was any way he could obtain a certain drug for seven children who would die without it. Dave wrote down the name of the drug and told the director that he had no idea how to get this type of drug. They then prayed over the phone and asked God to provide.

As Dave hung up the phone, before he even let go of the receiver, the phone rang again. It was a pharmaceutical company in New Jersey asking Dave if he would have any use for 48,000 vials of *that exact drug!* Not only did they offer him eight million dollars' worth of this drug, but they told him they would airlift it to anyplace in the world! Dave would later learn that the company was one of only two that manufactured this particular drug in the United States.

Within forty-eight hours, Dave had the drug sent to the treatment center in Honduras and to twenty other locations as well. It was then he believed firmly that God was at work, validating his calling to this ministry.

Year after year, God continues to provide supernaturally. Today they have distributed more than $950 million in food and other relief to more than ten million kids in seventy countries and thirty-two states. Children's Hunger Fund has distributed more than 150 million pounds of food and 110 million toys.

The uniqueness of CHF is that they train and equip volunteers from local churches to distribute the food through home deliveries in the United States and other countries. Going from family to family, they find the poorest of the poor and share not only food but love and the gospel. Forbes.com consistently rates CHF at the top of their list of America's most cost-effective charities.

One of the most beautiful things about this story is that if you met Dave, you would never think he was the CEO of a major organization. He is a quiet, soft-spoken man—not the type you envision leading a movement. His power doesn't necessarily come from a natural giftedness but from a dedicated prayer life. As a close, personal friend of Dave's, I don't know that I've ever spent time with him without spending time in prayer.

Dave lives a life we should long for and, incredibly, the kind of life that is offered to us as well. A life in which people know that our accomplishments could not have been attained by our own power. A life that brings glory to God in heaven.[4]

CHAPTER 7

Supernatural Church

*What the soul is in our body, the Holy Spirit is
in the body of Christ, which is the church.*

-Augustine-

I bet you'd agree that a group of talented, charismatic leaders can draw a crowd. Find the right creative team, musicians, and speakers, and you can grow any church. It doesn't even have to be a Christian church. The fact is that without making a conscious choice to depend on the Holy Spirit, we can do a lot. (Although without the Spirit, we wouldn't actually be drawing our next breath—but I am talking about cognizant and intentional dependence on our part.) My point is that a growing and energetic gathering is not necessarily evidence of the Holy Spirit's work.

We all have our natural talents and bents, things that we are "gifted at" (of course, the reality is that those gifts too are ultimately from God). I have friends who are gifted artists, and I love watching them paint and draw. Those of us who are artistically challenged are stunned by the beautiful works of art they create. Others are good with people and can easily work in a variety of jobs that require people skills. Still others know how to sell things, no matter what the product is. And some have the skill set required to pull off a decent church.

A while back I asked my church during a service if they thought I could successfully sell insurance as a career. I did this because I know that some of my natural skills are connected to interacting with people and speaking. The fact is that we all have jobs that come naturally for us. Because of how I was made, I could be an insurance salesman if I had a little bit of training. And I can probably "pull off" a fairly adequate church on my own as well. But who wants or needs that?

I don't want my life to be explainable without the Holy Spirit. I want people to look at my life and know that I couldn't be doing this by my own power. I want to live in such a way that I am desperate for Him to come through. That if He doesn't come through, I am screwed. (I probably shouldn't write that word here, but it's how I truly feel about this.)

There was a time when I got excited over a crowd showing up to hear me preach, but those days are long gone. Now I deeply desire that the Spirit of God would do things that I *know* are not of me and that cannot be faked or accounted for by human reason.

I don't believe God wants me (or any of His children) to live in a way that makes sense from the world's perspective, a way I know I can "manage." I believe He is calling me—and all of us—to depend on Him for living in a way that cannot be mimicked or forged. He wants us to walk in step with His Spirit rather than depend solely on the raw talent and knowledge He's given us.

But instead of living this way, we've created a whole brand of churches that do not depend on the Spirit, a whole culture of Christians who are not disciples, a new group of "followers" who do not follow. If all God asked for were faceless numbers to fill the churches, then we would all be doing all right. Most of us would feel pretty confident. But simply having a good speaker, a service that is short and engaging, a good venue, and whatever else we add to the mix does not make a "good" or "successful" church. God intended for His bride, those who claim His name, to be much more than this.

God is not interested in numbers. He cares most about the faithfulness, not the size, of His bride. He cares about whether people are lovers of Him. And while I might be able to get people in the doors of a church or auditorium if I tell enough jokes or use enough visuals, the fact remains that I cannot convince people to be obsessed with Jesus. Perhaps I can talk people into praying a prayer, but I cannot talk anyone into falling in love with Christ. I cannot make someone understand and accept the gift of grace. Only the Holy Spirit can do that. So by every measure that actually counts, I *need* the Holy Spirit. Desperately.

Sometimes I leave Christian events wondering if we resemble the prophets of Baal in 1 Kings 18 more than Elijah, the prophet of God.

If you've forgotten the story, it may be good to stop here and read that chapter, or else the rest of what I write in this section will make very little sense to you. The prophets of Baal had a loud, passionate worship gathering that lasted from morning till evening. When they were done, they had a great time of fellowship (I think you can call it that). But "no one answered; no one paid attention" (18:29). After all of that, Elijah prayed. God heard his prayer, and fire came down from heaven.

My favorite part of that story comes when it is all over and the prophets of Baal are saying, "The LORD—he is God! The LORD—he is God!" (18:39 NIV). They didn't say, "Elijah is a great speaker" or "Elijah sure knows how to connect with God!" They were stunned by *God*. They were in awe of His power. They knew that what they experienced could not have been manipulated by Elijah. They experienced the power of God.

Is that what happens at the Christian gatherings you attend? Or does it feel more like what the prophets of Baal experienced before Elijah prayed? We can have a great time singing and dancing ourselves into a frenzy. But at the end of it, fire doesn't come down from heaven. People leave talking about the people who led rather than the power of God.

This principle carries into the way we live our personal lives as well. People ought to see the transformation in our lives and respond by saying, "The Lord—He is God!"

Has anyone ever been amazed by your peace? Love? Joy? Have they ever envied your self-control? Have you ever prayed that God would so fill you with the Spirit that people would know the change could be empowered only by the Spirit? It is when we are filled with true peace and hope that people notice there is something different about us. The Holy Spirit is the one who gives us both peace (Rom. 14:17) and hope (15:13).

I think we all could agree that living "according to our sinful flesh" is not what is intended for us as children of God. Yet even so, we often choose to face life's issues and circumstances in exactly the same way as someone without the Spirit of God. We worry, strive, and grieve no differently than unbelievers. While it is true that we are humans like everyone else, it is also true that we are humans with the Spirit of God dwelling in us. Yet, whether consciously or not, we essentially say to God, "I know You raised Christ from the dead; but the fact is my problems are just too much for You and I need to deal with them by myself."

Even in our daily living we can look more like the prophets of Baal as we live our lives, running about in a frenzy, trying to fix our problems, not stopping long enough to call on the power of God Almighty. Yet as children of God, we are not called to trust in our idols or ourselves. We are made to be like Elijah, who did not question whether God would show His face that day. He prayed and asked for help, and God sent down fire from heaven in response.

Perhaps you don't need fire from heaven, but peace. Perhaps what you need is wisdom to know which decision to make. Or courage to do the right thing, even though you might lose your job. Or maybe you need love because you feel alone. Or you want people with a similar vision to journey with and support you along the way. Whatever you need, the point is that God is aware of you and your circumstances, and He knows what you really need. He is able to bring these things, people, and circumstances into your life.

But God is not a coercive God. And though He desires for His children to know peace and love and to have wisdom, I have noticed that often He waits for us to ask.

He desires to do more than "help out" a bit. He wants to completely transform us. He wants to take a timid heart and set it ablaze with strength and courage, so much so that people know something supernatural has taken place—life change just as miraculous as fire coming down from heaven. He wants to imbue us with His wisdom because He is the "spirit of wisdom and revelation" (Eph. 1:17; see Isa. 11:2). Even as the Spirit works in us to make us more like Christ, to transform us, He is also patient. This work will not be complete until His kingdom comes in full, though this does not deter Him from working now.

———

You are most likely familiar with the "fruit passage" in Galatians 5, which says, "But the fruit of the Spirit is love, joy, peace, patience, kindness, goodness, faithfulness, gentleness and self-control. Against such things there is no law" (vv. 22–23 NIV). You may even have the list memorized. But look over those traits right now and ask yourself if you possess each to a supernatural degree. Do you exhibit more kindness and faithfulness than the Mormons you know? Do you have more self-control than your Muslim friends? More peace than Buddhists? More joy than atheists? If GOD truly lives in you, shouldn't you expect to be different from everyone else?

What disturbs me most is when we're not really bothered that God living *in* us has not made much of a noticeable difference. Most churchgoers are content to find a bit of peace rather than a "peace of God, which surpasses all understanding" (Phil. 4:7). We want just enough peace to survive the week (or perhaps even the day).

Certainly there have been times in my life when just getting through the day was possible only with God's supernatural help and presence. You might understand the kind of desperate season I am talking about; most of us have experienced times like this—times when we really do have to ask for peace and sustenance every ten minutes. But what I am talking about is when we live our lives this way, when every day of our lives we are just barely hanging on, looking no different from the rest of the world.

When we exhibit the peace that surpasses the world's understanding, that's when the world notices. *That's* when people say, "Your Lord—He is God!"

—————

Now, this chapter is not meant to make you feel guilty. But it *is* meant to be a challenge and make a space for you to take an honest look at yourself. Do you know what it's like to be filled with joy? Do you experience genuine peace regardless of your life circumstances? Do you consistently respond with kindness no matter what you receive from others?

Can you imagine what it would be like never to get stressed-out or to worry because you are so filled with the peace and love of God?

Don't you want to be characterized by these attitudes? Don't we all want peace, and self-control, and all the rest?

Notice that the subject ("fruit") in this verse is singular. It does not say that there are many *fruits* of the Spirit, but that one fruit incorporates all the different elements that follow (love, joy, peace, etc.). This certainly doesn't make it any easier.

I don't know about you, but I cannot simply muster up more love. I can't manufacture patience just by gritting my teeth and determining to be more patient. We are not strong or good enough, and it doesn't work that way. None of us can "do goodness" on our own, much less all the other elements that make up the fruit of the Spirit.

But despite our inability to change ourselves in this way, to simply become more peaceful or joyful, we expend a great deal of effort trying. We focus on what God wants us to *do* and forget the kind of people He wants us *to be*.

Instead of mustering up more willpower, let's focus our energies and time on asking for help from the One who has the power to change us. Let's take the time to ask God to put the fruit of His Spirit into our lives. And let's spend time with the One we want to be more like.

I know in my own life I don't just want to do what my mentors do; I also want to spend time with them. I have found that through spending time with those I respect, I become more like them than I would by simply trying to "do what they do." Grunting and saying through clenched teeth, "I *will* be patient!" hasn't worked yet, and that isn't likely to change. But what does effect change is when we begin to ask God to make these fruit manifest in our lives, by the power of His Spirit, and when we spend time in communion with our God.

My favorite verse is quite possibly James 5:17, which reads, "Elijah was a man with a nature like ours, and he prayed fervently." Don't keep yourself from praying desperately and courageously for the Spirit to work in your life simply because you are not the prophet Elijah. As this verse says, Elijah was a human being with a nature like ours. He was just like us. The key thing about him? *He prayed fervently.*

Have you ever thought to yourself, "I'm praying to the exact same God Elijah prayed to"? Do you genuinely believe that Moses, Esther, David, and Daniel had *no* advantage over you spiritually? In fact, some would argue that you have the advantage of both the risen Christ and the indwelling Spirit. Let's stop looking at the godly men and women in Scripture as though their prayer lives are unattainable! Pray fervently, knowing that Peter and Paul and Mary and Ruth were men and women "with a nature like ours" (James 5:17). I know that I tend to run from situations where I *need* God, and I think that is true of almost every one of us. It is safer to avoid situations where we need God to come through than to stake it all on Him and risk God's silence. If Elijah had not had the courage to face down the prophets of Baal that day, if he hadn't prayed fervently and courageously, then he would not have experienced God's power in such a profound way. But in moments of doubt, I can't help but think, *What if God hadn't sent down fire that day and Elijah ended up in the same predicament as the prophets of Baal? What then?*

This is certainly not a call to demand that God prove Himself in each and every circumstance that we manufacture. But it is a profound reminder that God delights in showing up when His people are in desperate need of Him, because that means no one else can steal His glory.

Let's delve into the Old Testament once again and look at the story of Gideon in Judges 7. Gideon started with an army thirty-two thousand men strong. In several stages, God purposely dwindled it to three hundred men. I think God did this so that no one could say, "Look what we did!" Instead, everyone knew that it was God's power that defeated the enemy. Only through God could a tiny army of three hundred men rout the much larger Midianite army.

God wants the praise for what we do in our lives. But if we never pray audacious, courageous prayers, how can He answer them? If we never follow Him to positions where we need Him, how can He show up and make His presence known?

Can you, along with Elijah and Gideon, say that when people see your life they respond by praising our Father?

When I live by my own power and strength, relying solely on my natural talents to see me through, then people naturally praise me for how I am living. But when I am living in a way that requires me to depend on the Holy Spirit, people respond by praising my Father in heaven.

When was the last time you experienced the hand of God? Ask yourself. Think about the times in your life when you have been touched by God in a way that no one could convince you was a coincidence. These may not be "fire from heaven" or "voice like thunder" kinds of experiences; perhaps it was the wordless whisper of hope when you were overwhelmed by depression. Or perhaps you experienced God through the unconditional acceptance of another human being. Or maybe you glimpsed some of His character through a sunset that just made you stop and worship. We experience God through a variety of means, and God delights to communicate and share Himself with His beloved daughters and sons.

The Holy Spirit is present throughout the New Testament as well as the Old Testament. I believe in Him because I believe the Scriptures. But even if you took away what I "know" about the Holy Spirit from reading the Scriptures, my "right answers" about the Holy Spirit, I would still believe.

I would still believe in the Spirit because I have experienced God the Holy Spirit working in and through and around my life in ways I cannot deny or ignore. I certainly do not advocate ignoring the Scriptures or basing everything on experience, but to completely ignore experience—including your personal experience and the experience of the wider body of Christ, both now and historically—is unbiblical.

If you have not known and experienced God in ways you cannot deny, I would suggest that you are not living in a needy and dependent way. God delights to show up when His children call on His name and when they are trusting fully in Him to come through, whether that is in relationships, in battling sin, in strength to make sacrifices, or in endurance to be faithful in daily life. Are you living this way? Or are you surviving only by your own strength, by your own wits?

We Were Family

A while back a former gang member came to our church. He was heavily tattooed and rough around the edges, but he was curious to see what church was like. He had a relationship with Jesus and seemed to get fairly involved with the church.

After a few months, I found out the guy was no longer coming to the church. When asked why he didn't come anymore, he gave the following explanation: "I had the wrong idea of what church was going to be like. When I joined the church, I thought it was going to be like joining a gang. You see, in the gangs we weren't just nice to each other once a week—we were family." That killed me because I knew that what he expected is what the church is intended to be. It saddened me to think that a gang could paint a better picture of commitment, loyalty, and family than the local church body.

The church is intended to be a beautiful place of community. A place where wealth is shared and when one suffers, everyone suffers. A place where when one rejoices, everyone rejoices. A place where everyone experiences real love and acceptance in the midst of great honesty about our brokenness. Yet most of the time this is not even close to how we would describe our churches.

Without the Spirit of God in our midst, working in us, guiding us, and living and loving through us, we will never be the kind of people who make up this kind of community. There is no such thing as a real believer who doesn't have the Holy Spirit, or a real church without the Spirit. It's just not possible. But what is possible is that we would individually and corporately quench and hinder the Spirit's activity in and through our lives.

As for me, I am tired of talking about what we are going to do. I am sick of talking about helping people, of brainstorming and conferencing about ways we can be radical and make sacrifices. I don't want to merely talk anymore. Life is too short. I don't want to speak about Jesus; I want to know Jesus. I want to be Jesus to people. I don't want just to write about the Holy Spirit; I want to experience His presence in my life in a profound way.

———

A few months ago, the elders at Cornerstone Church began to ask the question "Why don't we live like the believers who made up the first church?" In Acts 2:42–47 we read the following:

> They devoted themselves to the apostles' teaching
> and to fellowship, to the breaking of bread and to
> prayer. Everyone was filled with awe at the many
> wonders and signs performed by the apostles. All
> the believers were together and had everything
> in common. They sold property and possessions
> to give to anyone who had need. Every day they
> continued to meet together in the temple courts.
> They broke bread in their homes and ate together
> with glad and sincere hearts, praising God and

enjoying the favor of all the people. And the Lord
added to their number daily those who were being
saved. (TNIV)

What followed was a beautiful time of sharing as our elders laid
"everything" at one another's feet. We surrendered the keys to our
cars, homes, and bank accounts. The elders looked me in the eyes
and said, "What's mine is yours. If anything ever happens to you, I
will support and care for your kids *as much as* I would care for my
own. I will be your life insurance." And because they had a history
of genuine sacrifice for the sake of the gospel, I believed what they
said.

From there, we began going to some of our friends in the
congregation and expressing our commitment to them. And now
this mentality is spreading. New life is permeating the church as
individuals back up their words with sacrifice. Cars and homes are
being sold or given away. Expensive vacations are joyfully replaced
with caring for others. People are being welcomed into others'
homes—not only for meals, but to live. This is a small example of
the kinds of things that happen when people start to walk with the
Spirit and ask the Holy Spirit to affect every part of their lives.

I just shared about what a few people in one church in one
city in one country are doing. What else might it look like when
people begin to walk with the Spirit, submitting everything to
Him? Dream a little with me. This will look different in various
cultures around the world. The Spirit will lead believers in Beijing
to do different things from believers in the United Kingdom or
Argentina.

This is just a hint of what happens when we begin to actually live like we need the Spirit. For us at Cornerstone Church, it is only the beginning.

Forceful or Forced?

When I read the book of Acts, I see the church as an unstoppable force. Nothing could thwart what God was doing, just as Jesus foretold: "The gates of hell shall not prevail against it" (Matt. 16:18). The church was powerful and spreading like wildfire, not because of clever planning, but by a movement of the Spirit. Riots, torture, poverty, or any other type of persecution couldn't stop it. Isn't that the type of church movement we all long to be a part of?

So much of what we see today is anything but unstoppable. It can easily be derailed by the resignation of a pastor or an internal church disagreement or budget cuts. Churches we build only by our own efforts and not in the strength of the Spirit will quickly collapse when we don't push and prod them along. I spent years asking God to be part of whatever I was doing. When I read the book of Acts, I see people privileged to play a part in what God was doing.

Recently we held a discussion about how to solve some of the evident problems in our church. One of our pastors spoke up and said, "I think we're trying too hard." He went on to share of the supernatural things that had taken place through his prayer life. At that point, we decided to stop talking and thinking. The next hour was spent intensely in prayer. We never got "back to business" that day. While there is a time to brainstorm and think and act well using the gifts God has given us, far too often we never get to prayer (much less start, end, and allow it to permeate all that we do). Let's pray that God would build His church, an unstoppable force, empowered and sustained by the Holy Spirit.

———————

No matter where you live and what your days look like, you have the choice each day to depend on yourself, to live safely, and to try to control your life. Or you can live as you were created to live—as a temple of the Holy Spirit of God, as a person dependent on Him, desperate for God the Spirit to show up and make a difference. When you begin living a life characterized by walking with the Spirit, that is when people will begin to look not to you but to our Father in heaven and give Him the praise.

My prayer as I've written this book is that it would not merely add to your knowledge. Maybe that sounds strange, but I mean it. Often in Christian circles we talk about truth in lieu of applying it to our lives. We hear an incisive sermon, discuss at lunch afterward how "great" or "powerful" it was, and then never think about it again, much less allow the Spirit to change us through it. The truth is that greater knowledge does not necessarily equal greater spirituality. Knowledge can lead to greater intimacy and a deeper relationship with God, but this is not an automatic effect.

Our Scriptures teach that if you know what you are supposed to do and you don't do it, then you sin (James 4:17). In other words, when we stock up on knowledge without applying it to our lives, we are actually sinning. You would think that learning more *about* God would be a good thing ... and it can be. But when we gain knowledge *about* God without responding *to* Him or assimilating His truth into our lives, then it is not a good thing. According to the Bible, it's sin.

May we not merely gain knowledge. Instead, as we learn, may we grow and confess and change more into the people we've been created to be by the power of the Holy Spirit, who dwells within us. "For the kingdom of God is not a matter of eating and drinking but of righteousness and peace and joy in the Holy Spirit" (Rom. 14:17).

The Final Biography

What if this last biography were about your life? What would be written here? Would we read stories about the indwelling work of the Holy Spirit or stories about what you have accomplished on your own? Don't be discouraged if there is not a lot of the Holy Spirit's working in your past. Pray in complete faith right now. Ask God to have His Spirit work so mightily in you that it would make for an amazing biography. A biography that speaks of a life so supernatural that no one would even consider giving you the glory. A biography that displays the power of the Spirit and lifts up the name of Jesus to the glory of God the Father. Amen.

AFTERWORD

My hope and prayer for you, the reader, is that church people don't try to normalize you. What I mean is that we often try to calm people down who are just too passionate or too sacrificial and radical. I know at times I have done this to other people. And I've had it done to me.

Two years ago at a dinner I sat next to a man who runs a human-trafficking awareness organization. He described how these children, most of whom were sold or abducted into the sex trade, are raped and abused every single night, again and again, how they have no one to advocate for them, and how there is no way out.

That night I lay awake in my bed for hours—literally hours—and I imagined my own children in this situation. Maybe that was a stupid thing to do, but suddenly, vividly, I was sobbing and I couldn't get the images out of my mind. I started thinking about what I would do if this really happened to my little girl. I know that I wouldn't stop until I had saved her. I would mobilize everyone I know through whatever means possible to get them to help. Lying there in my bed that night I got more and more passionate about everything I would do to save my little girl.

Then something happened. I am not one of those people who often hears God's distinct, clear voice (though I know some people do), but on this night, the Spirit of God said to me: *I want you to love them as your own children.* This was overwhelming to me. After all, if I treated these kids as though they were my own, I wouldn't stop praying for them. I also wouldn't stop passionately begging people to figure out ways to seek them out and rescue them. I literally wept for hours. The thought of these precious children of mine being taken advantage of was unbearable. I was now on a mission. A mission from God.

I remember getting back to Cornerstone and "rallying the troops." I was so fired up, and I got others fired up. But over the course of several months I got distracted. People around me started calming me down about sex trafficking. They said, "Francis, you can't save the world," and "You're already doing so much. Don't be so hard on yourself." And the passion I believe God gave me for children in the sex-slave trade slowly eked out of me.

Things like this happen all the time. As a church, we tend to do this to people who are passionate and bold. We mellow them out. Institutionalize them. Deaden them to the work that the Spirit is doing in them. In Acts 4:13 we read of the early church doing just the opposite. Peter and John testified before the Sanhedrin and "when they saw the courage of Peter and John and realized that they were unschooled, ordinary men, they were astonished and they took note that these men had been with Jesus" (NIV). The people were astonished at their courage and that they were uneducated. Right after Peter and John were released, they returned to the other believers and prayed for even more boldness and courage (4:29). Some of the boldest people (John and Peter) were the ones asking for more boldness!

Why don't we do this today? I have found that we generally do the opposite. Instead of encouraging people who are doing courageous things for God and joining them in their discernment process of how to be faithful to what God is calling them to, we tell them to slow down and back off. Instead of being astonished at believers' courage, frequently (and unfortunately) I am astonished at believers' timidity and lack of boldness. What a contrast to the biblical model we are given!

A few months ago I was speaking at a summer camp, and I was speaking to one of the organizations there that sponsors children. This volunteer told me about a sixteen-year-old girl there at the camp who sponsors fourteen children, on her own. I was astonished by this. Fourteen children (at about thirty dollars a month for each child) is a lot of money for a high school student to come up with. I talked to this girl and asked her how she did it. She told me that she works year-round and she works three jobs in the summertime to pay for the child support. While other teenagers are saving for a car, she's saving lives! Instead of spending her hard-earned money on herself and her future, she gives it to these fourteen children because she believes God loves them just as much as He loves her.

My prayer is that churchgoers will not dissuade her from this calling. That they won't tell her things like, "You really need to start thinking about yourself now. Your future and your education are important. What you've done is great, but it's time to think about what's next for you." Maybe this girl will stand strong in her conviction that the children she is supporting around the world are as important as she is … just maybe she won't be convinced out of her passionate love and sacrifice.

My wife and I recently decided to give all of the royalties from my previous book, *Crazy Love,* to the Isaiah 58 Fund. All of the money goes to the needy in the world—the starving, sick, impoverished, and to those in the sex-slave trade. We reasoned that if we kept all this money, we would end up spending it on things we didn't need. We knew that in the long run (eighty years from now), there would be no regrets. But if we bought things that wouldn't last beyond our time on earth, we would end up disappointed and regretful. I was a bit shocked and discouraged by some of the responses we received.

People told us that we were being foolish and irresponsible with the gifts God gave us. They said we should have at least put some away in case of an emergency. My response back was, "Is it not an emergency that children in Cambodia and Thailand and even the United States are being raped every single day of their lives? Why is that not an emergency?" I think the church often inadvertently teaches that the sex-slave trade is not an emergency. And this, I believe, is sin. Is an emergency only an emergency if it affects me and my immediate family?

I am not saying that every person is supposed to give all the money from their jobs to support children. Or that everyone has to create a fund from the royalties of their books. Or that each and every person is meant to get involved with organizations that work against the sex-slave trade. What I am saying, though, is that instead of thinking and telling people they are crazy when they feel like the Spirit is leading them into something that doesn't necessarily make sense to us, we should join them in the discernment process. Instead of discouraging people, we should pray for more insight and boldness. Instead of deadening people to the Spirit's leading with our words and our actions, we should celebrate and join the Spirit's movement in and through them!

This is not about one specific way of living radically. It is about discerning and obeying the Spirit's voice, especially when He asks you to do something that is hard, a little beyond "normal," and that requires sacrifice. This is a twofold thing: It is both about encouraging others to obey the Spirit's leadings and about listening to and obeying His leading in your own life. Do you feel bold and powerful? Whether your answer is yes or no, all of us need to ask for more courage and boldness.

So, finally, I just want to spend these last few paragraphs praying with you, the reader.

> *Spirit, we know that we have done wrong by You. Please forgive us for grieving, resisting, and quenching You. We have resisted You through sin, through our rebellion, and through our hardness of heart. At times, we have been spiritually blind. At other times, we knew what You wanted us to do, but we chose to ignore Your promptings. Yet this is not how we want to live now.*

We need You to change us. Only through You can we truly worship. Spirit of the Lord, You are the one who brings us to a place where we can worship. You are the Spirit of truth, the Spirit of holiness, the Spirit of life. Thank You for the truth, the holiness, and the life You give us.

We need Your wisdom and understanding as we seek to live this life. Keep us from disbelief, from fear. We need Your strength to help us do what you are asking us to do and to live how You are asking us to live. Speak loudly and drown out the other voices calling us to conform to the patterns of this world.

You are the Spirit of self-control and love. Give us the self-control needed to deny our flesh and follow You. Give us a love strong enough to motivate courageous action. Manifest Yourself through us that we may serve and love Your bride, the church, as You do.

Come, Holy Spirit, come. We don't know exactly what that means and looks like for each of us yet, in the particular places You've called us to inhabit. But, nonetheless, whatever it means, we ask for Your presence. Come, Holy Spirit, come.

NOTES

1. See www.JoniandFriends.org.

2. See www.Rationalpi.com/theshelter/ and www.Labri.org.

3. Esther Ahn Kim, *If I Perish* (Chicago: Moody Publishing, 2001).

4. See www.chfus.org.

ABOUT THE COAUTHOR

Danae Yankoski graduated from Westmont College, where she studied English Literature and met her best friend, now husband, Mike. An avid reader and writer from a young age, Danae has authored, coauthored, and contributed to several books including *Things I've Learned Lately*, *Crazy Love*, and *Zealous Love: A Guide to Social Justice*. Some of Danae's favorite aspects of life include mugs of tea and thought-provoking conversation; hiking, running, growing things, and being outside; interacting with different kinds of people; and playing with her black Lab, Elliott. She and Mike recently moved to Vancouver, BC, where they are pursuing their Masters of Christian Studies.

↓↑ crazy love

stop praying

What if I said, "Stop praying"? What if I told you to stop talking at God for a while, but instead to take a long, hard look at Him before you speak another word? Solomon warned us not to rush into God's presence with words. That's what fools do. And often, that's what we do.

We are a culture that relies on technology over community, a society in which spoken and written words are cheap, easy to come by, and excessive. Our culture says anything goes; fear of God is almost unheard of. We are slow to listen, quick to speak, and quick to become angry.

The wise man comes to God without saying a word and stands in awe of Him. It may seem a hopeless endeavor, to gaze at the invisible God. But Romans 1:20 tells us that through creation, we see His "invisible qualities" and "divine nature."

Let's begin this book by gazing at God in silence. What I want you to do right now is to go online and look at the "Awe Factor" video at www.crazylovebook.com to get a taste of the awe factor of our God. Seriously—go do it.

Speechless? Amazed? Humbled?

When I first saw those images, I had to worship. I didn't want to speak to or share it with anyone. I just wanted to sit quietly and admire the Creator.

It's wild to think that most of these galaxies have been discovered only in the past few years, thanks to the Hubble telescope. They've been in the universe for thousands of years without humans even knowing about them.

Why would God create more than 350,000,000,000 galaxies (and this is a conservative estimate) that generations of people never saw or even knew existed? Do you think maybe it was to make us say, "Wow, God is unfathomably big"? Or perhaps God wanted us to see these pictures so that our response would be, "Who do I think I am?"

R. C. Sproul writes, "Men are never duly touched and impressed with a conviction of their insignificance, until they have contrasted themselves with the majesty of God."[1]

↓↑

Switch gears with me for a minute and think about the detailed intricacy of the other side of creation.

Did you know that a caterpillar has 228 separate and distinct muscles in its head? That's quite a few, for a bug. The average elm tree has approximately 6 million leaves on it. And your own heart generates enough pressure as it pumps blood throughout your body that it could squirt blood up to 30 feet. (I've never tried this, and I don't recommend it.)

Have you ever thought about how diverse and creative God is? He didn't have to make hundreds of different kinds of bananas, but He did. He didn't have to put 3,000 different species of trees within one square mile in the Amazon jungle, but He did. God didn't have to create so many kinds of laughter. Think about the different sounds of your friends' laughs—wheezes, snorts, silent, loud, obnoxious.

How about the way plants defy gravity by drawing water upward from the ground into their stems and veins? Or did you know that spiders produce three kinds of silk? When they build their webs, they create sixty feet of silk in one hour, simultaneously producing special oil on their feet that prevents them from sticking to their own web. (Most of us hate spiders, but sixty feet an hour deserves some respect!) Coral plants are so sensitive that they can die if the water temperature varies by even one or two degrees.

Did you know that when you get goose bumps, the hair in your follicles is actually helping you stay warmer by trapping body heat? Or what about the simple fact that plants take in carbon dioxide (which is harmful to us) and produce oxygen (which we need to survive)? I'm sure you knew that, but have you ever marveled at it? And these same poison-swallowing, life-giving plants came from tiny seeds that were placed in the dirt. Some were watered, some weren't; but after a few days they poked through the soil and out into the warm sunlight.

Whatever God's reasons for such diversity, creativity, and sophistication in the universe, on earth, and in our own bodies, the point of it all is His glory. God's art speaks of Himself, reflecting who He is and what He is like.

> The heavens declare the glory of God; the skies proclaim the work of his hands. Day after day they pour forth speech; night after night they display knowledge. There is no speech or language where their voice is not heard. Their voice goes out into all the earth, their words to the ends of the world.
>
> —Psalm 19:1–4

This is why we are called to worship Him. His art, His handiwork, and His creation all echo the truth that He is glorious. There is no other like Him. He is the King of Kings, the Beginning and the End, the One who was and is and is to come. I know you've heard this before, but I don't want you to miss it.

I sometimes struggle with how to properly respond to God's magnitude in a world bent on ignoring or merely tolerating Him. But know this: God will not be tolerated. He instructs us to worship and fear Him.

Go back and reread the last two paragraphs. Go to the Web site www.crazylovebook.com and watch the "Just Stop and Think" fifteen-minute video. Close this book if you need to, and meditate on the almighty One who dwells in unapproachable light, the glorious One.

There is an epidemic of spiritual amnesia going around, and none of us is immune. No matter how many fascinating details we learn about God's creation, no matter how many pictures we see of His galaxies, and no matter how many sunsets we watch, we still forget.

Most of us know that we are supposed to love and fear God; that we are supposed to read our Bibles and pray so that we can get to know Him better; that we are supposed to worship Him with our lives. But actually living it out is challenging.

It confuses us when loving God is hard. Shouldn't it be easy to love a God so wonderful? When we love God because we feel we should love Him, instead of genuinely loving out of our true selves, we have forgotten who God really is. Our amnesia is flaring up again.

It may sound "un-Christian" to say that on some mornings I don't feel like loving God, or I just forget to. But I do. In our world, where hundreds of things distract us from God, we have to intentionally and consistently remind ourselves of Him.

I recently attended my high school reunion. People kept coming up to me and saying, "She's your wife?" They were amazed, I guess, that a woman so beautiful would marry someone like me. It happened enough times that I took a good look at a photograph of the two of us. I, too, was taken aback. It is astonishing that my wife chooses to be with me—and not just because she is beautiful. I was reminded of the fullness of what I have been given in my wife.

We need the same sort of reminders about God's goodness. We are programmed to focus on what we don't have, bombarded multiple times throughout the day with what we need to buy that will make us feel happier or sexier or more at peace. This dissatisfaction transfers over to our thinking about God. We forget that we already have everything we need in Him. Because we don't often think about the reality of who God is, we quickly forget that He is worthy to be worshipped and loved. We are to fear Him.

A. W. Tozer writes,

> What comes into our minds when we think about God is the most important thing about us.... Worship is pure or base as the worshiper entertains high or low thoughts of God. For this reason the gravest question before the Church is always God Himself, and the most portentous fact about any man is not what he at a given time may say or do, but what he in his deep heart conceives God to be like.[2]

If the "gravest question" before us really is what God Himself is like, how do we learn to know Him?

We have seen how He is the Creator of both the magnitude of the galaxies and the complexity of caterpillars. But what is He like? What are His characteristics? What are His defining attributes? How are we to fear Him? To speak to Him? Don't check out here. We need to be reminded of this stuff. It is both basic and crucial.

God is holy. A lot of people say that whatever you believe about God is fine, so long as you are sincere. But that is comparable to describing your friend in one instance as a three-hundred-pound sumo wrestler and in another as a five-foot-two, ninety-pound gymnast. No matter how sincere you are in your explanations, both descriptions of your friend simply cannot be true.

The preposterous part about our doing this to God is that He already has a name, an identity. We don't get to decide who God is. "God said to Moses, 'I am who I am'" (Ex. 3:14). We don't change that.

To say that God is holy is to say that He is set apart, distinct from us. And because of His set apart–ness, there is no way we can ever fathom all of who He is. To the Jews, saying something three times demonstrated its perfection, so to call God "Holy, Holy, Holy" is to say that He is perfectly set apart, with nothing and no one to compare Him to. That is what it means to be "holy."

Many Spirit-filled authors have exhausted the thesaurus in order to describe God with the glory He deserves. His perfect holiness, by definition, assures us that our words can't contain Him. Isn't it a comfort to worship a God we cannot exaggerate?

God is eternal. Most of us would probably agree with that statement. But have you ever seriously meditated on what it means? Each of us had a beginning; everything in existence began on a particular day, at a specific time.

Everything, that is, but God. He always has been, since before there was an earth, a universe, or even angels. God exists outside of time, and since we are within time, there is no way we will ever totally grasp that concept.

Not being able to fully understand God is frustrating, but it is ridiculous for us to think we have the right to limit God to something we are capable of comprehending. What a stunted, insignificant god that would be! If my mind is the size of a soda can and God is the size of all the oceans, it would be stupid for me to say He is only the small amount of water I can scoop into my little can. God is so much bigger, so far beyond our time-encased, air/food/sleep–dependent lives.

Please stop here, even if just for a moment, and glorify the eternal God: "But you, O LORD, sit enthroned forever; your renown endures through all generations.... But you remain the same, and your years will never end" (Ps. 102:12, 27).

God is all-knowing. Isn't this an intimidating thought?

Each of us, to some degree, fools our friends and family about who we really are. But it's impossible to do that with God. He knows each of us, deeply and specifically. He knows our thoughts before we think them, our actions before we commit them, whether we are lying down or sitting or walking around. He knows who we are and what we are about. We cannot escape Him, not even if we want to. When I grow weary of trying to be faithful to Him and want a break, it doesn't come as a surprise to God.

For David, God's knowledge led him to worship. He viewed it as wonderful and meaningful. He wrote in Psalm 139 that even in the darkness he couldn't hide from God; that while he was in his mother's womb, God was there.

Hebrews 4:13 says, "Nothing in all creation is hidden from God's sight. Everything is uncovered and laid bare before the eyes of him to whom we must give account." It is sobering to realize that this is the same God who is holy and eternal, the Maker of the billions of galaxies and thousands of tree species in the rainforest. This is the God who takes the time to know all the little details about each of us. He does not have to know us so well, but He chooses to.

God is all-powerful. Colossians 1:16 tells us that everything was created for God: "For by him all things were created: things in heaven and on earth, visible and invisible, whether thrones or powers or rulers or authorities; all things were created by him and for him."

Don't we live instead as though God is created for us, to do our bidding, to bless us, and to take care of our loved ones?

Psalm 115:3 reveals, "Our God is in heaven; he does whatever pleases him." Yet we keep on questioning Him: "Why did You make me with this body, instead of that one?" "Why are so many people dying of starvation?" "Why are there so many planets with nothing living on them?" "Why is my family so messed up?" "Why don't You make Yourself more obvious to the people who need You?"

The answer to each of these questions is simply this: because He's God. He has more of a right to ask us why so many people are starving. As much as we want God to explain himself to us, His creation, we are in no place to demand that He give an account to us.

> All the peoples of the earth are regarded as nothing.
> He does as he pleases with the powers of heaven
> and the peoples of the earth. No one can hold back
> his hand or say to him: "What have you done?"

—Daniel 4:35

Can you worship a God who isn't obligated to explain His actions to you? Could it be your arrogance that makes you think God owes you an explanation?

Do you really believe that compared to God, "all the peoples of the earth are regarded as nothing," including you?

God is fair and just. One definition of justice is "reward and/or penalty as deserved." If what we truly deserved were up to us, we would end up with as many different answers as people who responded. But it isn't up to us, mostly because none of us are good.

God is the only Being who is good, and the standards are set by Him. Because God hates sin, He has to punish those guilty of sin. Maybe that's not an appealing standard. But to put it bluntly, when you get your own universe, you can make your own standards. When we disagree, let's not assume it's His reasoning that needs correction.

It takes a lot for us to comprehend God's total hatred for sin. We make excuses like, "Yes, I am prideful at times, but everyone struggles with pride." However, God says in Proverbs 8:13, "I hate pride and arrogance." You and I are not allowed to tell Him how much He can hate it. He can hate and punish it as severely as His justice demands.

God never excuses sin. And He is always consistent with that ethic. Whenever we start to question whether God really hates sin, we have only to think of the cross, where His Son was tortured, mocked, and beaten because of sin. Our sin.

No question about it: God hates and must punish sin. And He is totally just and fair in doing so.

Before the Throne

So far we have talked about things we can see with our own eyes, things we know about creation, and some of the attributes of God as revealed in the Bible. But many facets of God expand beyond our comprehension. He cannot be contained in this world, explained by our vocabulary, or grasped by our understanding.

Yet in Revelation 4 and Isaiah 6 we get two distinct glimpses of the heavenly throne room. Let me paint a bit of a word picture for you.

In Revelation, when John recounts his experience of seeing God, it's as though he's scrambling for earthly words to describe the vision he was privileged to see. He describes the One seated on the throne with two gems, "jasper and carnelian," and the area around the throne as a rainbow that looked like an emerald. God, the One on the throne, resembles radiant jewels more than flesh and blood.

This sort of poetic, artistic imagery can be difficult for those of us who don't think that way. So imagine the most stunning sunset you've ever seen. Remember the radiant colors splashed across the sky? The way you stopped to gaze at it in awe? And how the words wow and beautiful seemed so lacking? That's a small bit of what John is talking about in Revelation 4 as he attempts to articulate his vision of heaven's throne room.

John describes "flashes of lightning" and "rumblings and peals of thunder" coming from God's throne, a throne that must be unlike any other. He writes that before the throne are seven blazing torches and something like a sea of glass that looks like crystal. Using ordinary words, he does his best to describe a heavenly place and a holy God.

Most intriguing to me is how John describes those who surround the throne. First, there are the twenty-four elders dressed in white and wearing golden crowns. Next, John describes four six-winged beings with eyes all over their bodies and wings. One has the face of a lion, one of an ox, one of a man, and one of an eagle.

I try to imagine what it would be like if I actually saw one of these creatures out in the woods or down at the beach. I would probably pass out! It would be terrifying to see a being with the face of a lion and eyes "all around and within."

As if John's description isn't wild and strange enough, he then tells us what the beings are saying. The twenty-four elders cast their gold crowns before the One on the throne, fall on their faces before Him, and say, "You are worthy, our Lord and God, to receive glory and honor and power, for you created all things, and by your will they were created and have their being." At the same time, the four creatures never stop (day or night) saying, "Holy, holy, holy is the LORD God Almighty, who was, and is, and is to come!" Just imagine being in that room, surrounded by the elders chanting God's worth, and the creatures declaring God's holiness.

The prophet Isaiah also had a vision of God in His throne room, but this time it is a more direct picture: "I saw the Lord seated on a throne."

Wow. Isaiah saw that and lived? The Israelites hid themselves whenever God passed by their camp because they were too afraid to look at Him, even the back of Him as He moved away. They were scared they would die if they saw God.

But Isaiah looked and saw God. He writes that the bottom of God's robe filled the whole temple, and that the seraphim appeared above Him. The seraphim each had six wings, similar to the creatures John describes in Revelation. Isaiah says they called out to one another, saying, "Holy, holy, holy is the Lord Almighty; the whole earth is full of his glory!" Then the foundations shook and smoke filled the house, which is similar to John's description of flashes of lightning and peals of thunder.

Isaiah's description is less detailed than John's, but Isaiah shares more of his response to being in the throne room of God. His words reverberate in the wake of the smoky room and shaky foundation: "Woe is me.... I am ruined! For I am a man of unclean lips, and my eyes have seen the King, the Lord Almighty." And then one of the seraphim brings Isaiah a piece of burning coal that had been smoldering on the altar. The creature touches Isaiah's mouth with the hot coal and tells him that his guilt is taken away.

Both of these descriptions serve a purpose. John's helps us imagine what the throne room of God looks like, while Isaiah's reminds us what our only response to such a God should be.

May Isaiah's cry become our own. Woe is me ... we are a people of unclean lips!

Perhaps you need to take a deep breath after thinking about the God who made galaxies and caterpillars, the One who sits enthroned and eternally praised by beings so fascinating that were they photographed, it would make primetime news for weeks. If you are not staggered, go to Isaiah 6 and Revelation 4 and read the accounts aloud and slowly, doing your best to imagine what the authors describe.

The appropriate way to end this chapter is the same way we began it—by standing in awed silence before a mighty, fearsome God, whose tremendous worth becomes even more apparent as we see our own puny selves in comparison.

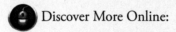Discover More Online:

www.ForgottenGod.com

www.BasicSeries.com